MANAGE LYMPHATICALLY

Sheri DuBois

Manage Lymphatically

Published by Spines

ISBN: 979-8-89383-008-8

MANAGE LYMPHATICALLY
PHYSIOLOGY OF PRACTICAL DECISION-MAKING

SHERI DUBOIS

CONTENTS

FOREWORD

"Vincit qui se vincit," reads the largest whiteboard. Written in orange whiteboard pen, in 2017, my favorite person wrote it for my favorite person's High School graduation party. We celebrated Cael's exceptional accomplishments, displaying her talented artwork at Total Health in La Junta, Colorado. Cael has taught life lessons that I was not certain were surmountable. My time during the previous few decades was formally focused on her crowned brilliant mind and beautiful radiance. Secondarily, I was invested in the development of a comprehensive yet simple bodywork style and personal brand, soft tissue recovery (str). In both a physical and physiological manner, I was often engaging life in a squint while attempting to heal another layer or new injury. This journey inspired nurturing change.

Tertiarily, I invested ten years to darn an academic participation crown. This author's research in middle management unexpectedly supported long-standing clinical findings in health. At a point when I was looking to transition from a hands-on trade to professional writing and research, obstacles to a successfully smooth transition presented themselves regularly. Through dedicated analysis, the clinical and academic obstacles appeared to repeatedly mirror or mimic one another, regardless of the stark differences in culture and environment. Pleasantly, positive engagement proved to reinforce the vast value of our human potential. My gut, my heart, and my mind were lit ablaze. I was suddenly in love with myself again. Faith in humanity surged. My faith in you surged.

Cael was right. I decided to publish shelved doctoral progress in a narrative form and include the academic progress as supporting documentation without formal supervision of university support. As the years unfolded, the clinical Mission Statement of my healing shop came to life. Clearly and discernably, with specific points of confirmation, this author learned to rely upon homeostatic responses to stimuli in management for best decision-making practices. More concisely, I learned to best live after coining this term and learning to: optimize physiological efficiency (ope).

Styling a personal brand, str, in 2006 was a professional move launched upon a student challenge while teaching Massage Therapy at a local Junior College. Through family life, academic degrees, occupational interests, and great focus, str came to my shop, Total Health. Most people I met needed to recover their health before they were able to optimize, while daily life allowed little external nurture to do so. People were making poor decisions while taxing personal homeostasis, the very health balance that provides for optimized decision-making. My life's work has been proven by you: we do heal properly when required to properly healing. There is only one thing for me to do. Through acute decision-making skills, I decided to share a passion, and I welcome formal or casual responses. I am interested in how my life branding may assist your longevity through the body-knowledge approach; this is my personal interest. Professionally, I present a thoughtful narrative I hope provides you with a benefit or two for your own personal decision-making practices.

Manage Lymphatically: Decision-Making Skills during Change and Culture Development for Inclusive Equity as Diverse Organizational Policy Incorporates Optimizing Physiological Efficiency

by Sheri DuBois

PROLOGUE

I am Impossible. I am a Giver. I am willing to Take: charge; your time; my time; your input into consideration; precedence; action; your hand in mine; voluntary vegan meals of pleasant flavor; steps on our Stairway to Heaven, tour Earth Eden with new eyes, and to Take-on a fresh perspective. What I am willing to take is not intended to hurt you. There are many factors to consider when engaging in intentional decision-making skills aimed at optimizing a culture of both inclusion and efficiency. We practice purposeful intent, heightening organizational efficiencies daily. Change is purposeful in the title, although elaboration on change is taken as an expectation in this writing.

Our world changes. Organizations change or adapt with cultural nurturing and external influence, often leading to greater inclusion as the outcome. Decision-making is a direct, consciously circumstantial manifestation of change. Witnessing one's decision-making influence through inclusion reinforces efficiency practices as teams proverbially bounce ideas off one another. Change remains at the forefront of navigating management as a condition of the requirement for management. Enjoy your review; your reflections are encouraged and appreciated.

Four main tenets to my personal challenges have impacted organizational plans and also instilled within me a personal expectation for change in these four tenets: pain, academics, athleticism, and care. Pain became my motivation for what now has become a two-part brand; I learned to assist folks out of their own a bit then, too. Academics became a pathway for broader and more specific conversations to a global bridge. Athleticism remains a preferred marker, a methodological approach to analyze bodywork practices in personal function and efficiency. Care is my cornerstone. I care to share the value that has been helpful to me. These tenets are the framework I utilize in working with folks over decades, learning and developing a personal approach to living fluid leadership.

Organizational managers expect compensation for successfully navigating opportunities and threats to best satisfy product and service demands. Reliable decision-making is an asset and the reason I developed a strategy for critical positions over the years. Within organizations that promote career longevity, competent managers may attract greater personal benefits and lower personal threats to their position with continued participation in ongoing organizational successes. Organizational gains may then, in return, create a manager's desire to perform at continued elevation. Consider this as a reference to constant gains from a previous quarter as an example. Success without ebbs, or constant strain on organizational homeostasis, contributes to potentially detrimental management behaviors when organic personal limitations are repeatedly taxed in decision-making until these skills weaken and then diminish.

Limitations may be surpassed with discipline and organic stress management tools - focused intent, visualization, breath, and movement. In my experience, exhaustively insistent demands through inorganic or unfamiliar stimuli may be motivational, but if I do not feel my efforts are organic and effective, I do not see the point in my participation. The effectiveness of organic management tools on decision-making processes for efficient physiological discernment, or the acceptance and repulsion of perceived data through the personal efforts of organizational management, is presented for ongoing considerations. Allow me to introduce physiological research from a narrative perspective. The dissertation journey has been an inspiring ten years focused on practical decision-making skills.

CHAPTER ONE

DECISIONS IN MANAGEMENT

Reliable decision-making at any time may appear natural for some leadership that comes to mind from the reader's experience. It may be witnessed that leadership decisions become more reliably honed over time. In the history of leadership, there is no more efficient humbling mechanism than an intelligent force of individuals with access to real-time data. Today, at this time, which provides an immense amount of information available, leaders find themselves incorporating dynamic tangible and intangible data processing through innate and learned managerial skills. The focus of this research pivots on the assumption that a leader in force today also manages competent leaders.

For reasons of inclusion, leaders and managers of varying experience are referred to in this work as management. Although leadership is not management, leaders often self-manage temperament, health, energy, and revitalization. Self-management throughout decision-making enhances the leadership effect. While breath and body movement hold significant benefits to team productivity for revitalization exercises and mental clarity, this research includes intentional visualization and assessment of an individual's optimum rejuvenation techniques. In the same manner that an organization's environmental impact team may aim for specific goals and fall short when a team member doesn't make the connection at the appropriate time and place, decision-making is impeded when one physiological system is taxed or inefficiently operating.

This last principle operates at independent thresholds. Individual physiological responses vary with circumstantial demands. Still, when one's threshold has been surpassed, effective decision-making is relentlessly diminished regardless of experience. The premise of this author's research settles ongoing debates for proponents of extreme theory within management ranks. Organizational theories from executive to labor workforce may reinforce an extreme culture when people are placed over production or production is placed over people. In this author's experience, optimum organizational efficiency is more complicated than the application of an operating theory. The complexity involves one's ability to self-manage and manage the self-management of those on organizational teams.

Intuitive managerial moments provide an experiential framework used in decision-making, from seconds-count decisions to decades of success and failure based on the impact of a decision. The impact of a decision builds and repeats generation upon generation, both in personal and professional living. Regulatory proceedings, legislation, and generations of qualified professionals explain how to best define success and where failure germinates as an individual. Defining success or failure is simple through third-party observation. Meanwhile, most management means to improve a situation through attuned profiteer antennae; they may also misunderstand available resources and potential limits of a workforce. A profiteering manager who gains legitimate support within a resource-limited hierarchy does so based on the expectation of personal compensation envisioned by those responsibly engaged.

Responsibility within an organization spans all roles. Executive roles take fiscal and cultural responsibility; workforce execution takes safety and production or service responsibility. Managers provide the common language for bridging linguistic competence between echelons, often depicting to a workforce how, why, when, and where to apply an execution of an executive decision. Managers further determine the level of efficiency for multi-echelon competency utilization and inter-departmental dependencies. Based on the author's experience, decision research for traditional military and business structures is used throughout this paper to frame physiological awareness in writing that is familiar to the reader. The level of research presented here is not limited to hierarchical entities. Competing variables influence decisions; the managerial mass of today's organization has often received guidance or at least been handed a training book in useful decision-making skills.

Management may hold higher educational degrees and be versed in decision-making successes and failures, though not all hold results from analysis on long-term impact. Well-planned organizations may fail when personnel know what to do but not how, diminishing execution from a lack of self-awareness. Understanding self, managers realize personal influence (or non-influence) on the organization while optimizing learned management skills that are personally effective. Preferably, culture is instilled through leadership, honored by organizational structure, vision, and strategy – recognizable and actionable by personnel.

CHAPTER TWO

VISCERAL MANAGEMENT

Long-term success relies upon structures and strategies that honor the dedication of top-performing managers who continuously hone skill sets for competitive productivity. The one small element mentioned above is a visceral knowledge of self, a skill set of top managers, and an ability to apply knowledge with awareness beyond the grasp of capture while in action. These are the managers whose decisions are rarely questioned, their direction rarely detoured; this ability to manage brought awareness to the world of transparent, transformative hope. Imagine this hope springs from a true and pure relationship with actionable knowledge, a possession of knowing that may not be separated from a person. In The Metaphysical Elements of Right, Immanuel Kant discusses individual rights of property as direct physical possession with external possessions reliant upon civil agreement and communal soil possession (Reiss (ed.), p.136). Managers who choose to honor the direct physical possession of these human gifts provide hope regardless of external possession.

Hope breeds through humanistic, social, political, and economic reforms geared toward helping billions within the workforce achieve a safe and satisfying compensatory work environment. Hope is relevant to organizational adhesion while experiencing personal and professional change cycles. The managers providing this hope are authentic, honest, and trustworthy; the data utilized in exceptional management is unique, guaranteed, and trainable, and objects are not sufficiently gathered. Data is gathered in real-time as optimized decision-making results in reinforcing an optimized culture. Objectives used to teach this form of visceral, fluid management are not adequately documented; the ability to teach this managerial element without documentation is limited to motivation.

Accountability in Decisions

Motivation coupled with personal accountability becomes a force; successful motivation positively affects the physiology of personnel, directly impacting life decisions – work and home. Physiological implications for organizational and human resilience embrace personal awareness and responsibility in decision-making, as addressed throughout the next chapter. Recognizing another person's workplace contribution reduces stress as each applies effort toward optimizing performance within unique scopes of practice and spheres of responsibility. A sense of personal and organizational success is gained from efficient duty completion and taking personal responsibility for one's sphere of influence within the organization. Acknowledging that all participants contributed to the final wrap-up of a project is reassuring and minimizes perceived workplace threat to the individual. Workplace threat is a silent intrapersonal communication of perceived threat to an individual, regardless of the intended attention from others.

The personal threat has an immediate impact on the level of trust and spontaneity of honest creativity applied to one's occupational responsibility in the form of standard performance. Standard performance deviates only from the common pivot of duty variance, experience, and skill set separate organizational duties (Tjosvold, 1987), while overall objectives remain. In other words, the welder is not repairing software; still, the welder benefits, is satisfied and feels a mutual sense of relief when the software is operational again. The welder did not have the responsibility, yet the achieved success belonged to all; personnel hold varying responsibilities of an objective, reliant upon one another's responsibilities. Although temporary, missed deadlines create visceral stress, and completed objectives create inclusive accomplishment.

Workplace Stress

It is perceived stress, on the whole, which promotes individual threat and impacts trust. Performance varies even when expectations are defined with measurable evaluation; this is an opportunity for organizations to improve or improvise to minimize threats and increase trust. Organizational goals and efficiency rely upon cooperative operations, creating a collective consciousness and culture of participation dependent on commitment to solution orientation. Both experience and skill sets provide enough vitality to encourage personalization or personality influence, creating a personal translation of duty performance for the same description (Gerhardt, Ashenbaum, & Newman, 2009). A simple example: one manager completes performance evaluations weekly with an appreciative staff, no surprises, while another manager performs only mandated evaluations. The latter manager also has an appreciative staff due to his personal belief that evaluations limit personnel creativity and potential; an observer may say both of these managers are wrong. There remains discord in participation due to competitive positioning, which allows people to question one another's effectiveness (Tjosvold, 1987, p. 742).

Successful interactions foster open disagreement accountable at the appropriate level of responsibility without evoking right or wrong persuasion (p. 747). Examples of right or wrong persuasion that become indoctrinated through policy include the logistical optimization of post-mail delivery, inter-departmental or external. When mail is delivered internally, given the option, one manager may opt for a central delivery system and another for departments to develop intra-departmental plans such as additional duties. Department managers in the latter can opt to have a rotating duty schedule for picking up mail (great for stagnant work operations) or one designated and certified internal mail courier. In this example, the managers have one duty description, yet each interprets what may generically read as "…, manages mail delivery, …" for logistical department efficiency. Differences are strengths; understanding the self within the department or organization provides relational cues with external interactions to create a physiological response. Leaders account for unacceptable professional behaviors with boundaries; in contrast, leaders discover positivity by unbinding restrictive doctrine.

Physiological Awareness

Gut-level cues provide insight into simple performance assessment voids; personnel development requires trained guidance and unlimited leadership insight on potentials. Providing a work environment that allows for creativity while containing negative professional behaviors optimizes personnel contribution with enhanced personal awareness. Today's workforce engages in either purposeful occupational careers or works for the money and picks up a paycheck; both are acceptable, and both are encouraged for specific operations. There is a challenge presented when disengaged personnel results in high turn-over rates; without an efficient method for countering turn-over, managers continually develop new personnel. Some managers are more efficient in this skill set than others, and the development of longevity in new trainees who desire this self-aware decision-making builds curiosity and loyalty. New phenomenology of physiological performance systems led research to the central question of whether physiological training is beneficial in developing decision-making efficiency.

Physiological Management

The body of knowledge in management aims to research the psychological training impact, and further research is needed in the field of physiological training and management. Physiological motivation is a side-effect of successful psychological or motivational training for leading skills in motivation to engage physiological assimilation for heightened work-related focus. Assimilating physiological responses creates personal responsibility for job performance where focus decreases due to strain on individual resilience, decision-making, and self-regulation abilities. Cross-disciplinary literature identifies a gap between physiological awareness and a direct and significant impact on the above performance skills when optimizing job performance. There is a gap between psychological motivators and physiological motivators that is only accessible through choice and an individual sense of purpose. The central question qualitatively focuses on whether physiological awareness training or autonomy has a beneficial impact on organizational efficiency. The use of physiological cues and self-care tools for autonomous human resource resiliency training is quantitatively hypothesized to be positively pertinent to organizational efficiency.

CHAPTER THREE

LITERATURE REVIEW
INTRODUCTION

Current research provides compelling evidence that effective decision-making and resilience through high-demand duty performance also involve managing physiological markers. The current body of knowledge contextually drives organizational management and development with little accountability of physiological understanding as long as essential jobs are managed. Risk exists when performance and workplace attitudes succeed while thoughtful, personal contributions fall to the impact of a quiet void. Narrowing reliable research during the initial phases of physiological management awareness reinforces established concepts, building onto a continuum of refined and evolving research. Effective organizational decisions rely on thorough collaboration of individual decision-making capacities. Reliable data requires scrutiny and respect for the knowledge or experience of replicable patterns leading physiological management through an early-staged proposition. The topic of physiological management involves a body consciousness separate from the mind. Review of thousands of articles provided little evidence of autonomous body consciousness, the research expands in scope to include a body intelligence (Hyland, 2002). The evident inclusion of conscious or intellectual influence from the body in relation to performance and decision-making efficiency continues to grow.

The central question is two-fold: whether physiological training develops more successful decision-making skills and whether this awareness positively impacts organizational efficiency. First, evidence proposes a physiological response provides cumulative learned adaptability (Mintzberg, 2009, p. 56) capable of increasing awareness of decision-making skills. Adaptive learning utilizes individual awareness training as a motivational tool for today's change management needs; developing people increases standard organizational efficiencies. Developing people and creating efficient organizational standards lead toward more consistent decision-making processes and enhancing a leader's decision-making effectiveness. These processes and related skills impact all organizational levels where consistent, effective decision-making processes further depend upon personal discipline. Individual discipline is susceptible to physiological fluctuations known as depletion management that functionally limit decision-making capacity (Inzlicht & Schmeichel, 2012). Depletion affects duty performance with cycles ranging from high-functioning to drowsy or asleep; the level of function an individual possesses is a matter of physiological awareness.

Physiological awareness is a personal measure, commonly described as visceral knowing or gut instinct; developing this awareness constitutes the central question's training goal. Willful discipline is accessible in a variety of forms, though the most efficient methods provide a dual benefit, allowing the individual to also manage the depletion of physiological resources. A personal willingness to develop self-discipline for recognizing physiological awareness assists in higher levels of attentiveness despite fluctuations in organizational demand (Batorski, 2012). One's desire to address personal needs within unconventional timeframes may appear organizationally detrimental or a costly inconvenience. Instead, regaining higher-level function is instantaneous when nurtured, providing enhanced duration of focused individual contribution to the organization (Batorski, 2012). Given the opportunity to reflect for three minutes enhances one's willingness to function with a competitive edge over someone in a high-function state yet an unwilling disposition (DeWall, Baumeister, Gailliot, & Maner, 2008; Gerhardt, 2009).

Second to the central question is whether training people on physiological awareness creates a measurable positive impact on organizational efficiency. Establishing a practice of physiological awareness training could have a positive, a negative, or a neutral impact on organizational efficiency, depending on assimilation interpretation. Considering elements of workforce burnout, enhanced personal awareness could negatively impact organizational efficiency as employees become more acutely aware of stress risk. The risk of stress is countered through resiliency. Individual resilience relies upon the physiological management of depletion as described above and trained through physiological awareness in practical steps (Inzlicht & Schmeichel, 2012). Depletion-management research incorporates simple steps to regain mental acuity utilizing physiological awareness cues or markers, such as slowed or diminished thinking processes. Employment of depletion-management practices then becomes personal responsibility through developing physiological awareness that is responsive to organizational demands.

Carefully targeted research provides insight into practical organizational steps for efficiency when risks are managed; awareness, willfulness, and resilience impact duty. Military preparedness training develops willfulness in the dynamic human resource. Integration and assimilation of new information during phases of change rely upon cognitive differentiation; people under stress diminish new information to simply news (Fautua & Schatz, 2012). Threat perceived at the workplace diminishes personal efficiency although this perception is individual and not a group endeavor perception (Dickerson, Gable, Irwin, et. al, 2009). Limited engagement in organizational resource management and growth challenges theorists and practitioners in identifying constructive interactive behavioral patterns (Tjosvold, 1987, p. 746). Decades of management and research lend a thread of truth in principled leadership, taking personal responsibility for the impact and acceptance of decision-making outcomes. Greater personal awareness and preparedness are anticipated to positively impact overall organizational efficiency.

Background

Five pieces of contextual literature involve physiology – or unknown psychological influences – which further impact organizational development with physiologically related roles. The influence of physiology is pertinent in recovering from work-related stress and personal demands that impede health in a variety of physiological failures, as do electric circuits. Two of these physiological re-set points are referred to as ego-depletion (Inzlicht & Schmeichel, 2012) and self-efficacy (Awadzi Calloway, 2010); each challenges organizational performance by interfering with decision-making skills. Psychologically, the consistently reliable unconscious (de Vries, Witteman, Holland & Dijksterhuis, 2010) and the intuitive element (McNaught, 2012) perform as alternative decision-makers from the conscious mind, commonly relied upon as the primary source. Assimilating the four elements of decision-making performance remains less focused on ability; an individual's willingness to perform more reliably provides immediate and functional results (Gerhardt, 2009). Additional seminal theoretical research rests squarely on the transparency of individual intent and collaborative learning, honoring essential elements of ethical humanism (CITI, 2012).

Six additional pieces of seminal theoretical research reinforce organizational ethics' inclusion of physiology or unknown psychological influences analyzed on baseline behavioral data. Understanding body consciousness incorporates conscious efforts exercised for developing awareness of self and recognizing an internal environment relative to externally perceived scenarios. Developing cognitive internal and external environmental relativity further requires mind recognition, which taxes the brain yet develops higher function and situational awareness (Batorski, 2012). Situational awareness is irrelevant when the external awareness is not met or matched with a competent internal bearing for an appropriate activity or response. Creating synergistic potential between situational awareness and appropriate use of self as a tool (article at the office) evolves by practice in regulating self-behavior and duty performance. Self-regulation defines an autonomous physiological impact on behavior as direct regulatory practice impacting organizationally specific duty performance needed to perform daily tasks (DeWall, Baumeister, Gailliot & Maner, 2008). Regulating self provides increasingly consistent reliability for determining one critical element affecting organizational efficiency, the human resource. Environments supporting the awareness and practice of individual resiliency skills clarify organizational goals and goal competencies that are personally and physiologically managed.

The last three of these six seminal theoretical research articles encourage broader acceptance of the influence on socially constructed organizational behaviors. Social construct is reliant upon collaborative perspective, accurate information is subject to influence of both social and biological impulse such as mirror neurons questioning true objectivity (Jaffe, 2007).

Duty completion or progress and the sense of personal and organizational success standards deviate from commonality through individual experience and skill set variance (Tjosvold, 1987). Foundational respect for whole-organization integrity is a baseline expectation in dealing with or discussing personnel, encouraging participation, and addressing adversity (p. 744). Individuals assimilate organizational efforts toward addressing common goals, reaching complex levels of organizational consciousness needs the person in order to ensure integration. Organizational consciousness collaboratively shifts toward efficiency by looking through and beyond the obvious to unmet organizational needs (Pees, Shoop & Ziegenfuss, 2009).

The most important recent seminal theoretical research-based literature includes altruistic behaviors providing clues to long-term success under strategically styled management (Sosik, Jung, & Dinger, 2009). Performance parameters within eight basic dimensions are discussed further in relation to physiology and intent on sustaining excellence through wisdom, as well as value the ongoing human drive (Talwar, 2011). Human drive requires physiological assimilation with action; the proactive personality efficiently utilizes self-management (Gerhardt, Ashenbaum, & Newman, 2009). Directed attention provides restoration in stress and depletion where self-regulation tolls on management's capabilities, clarifying prioritization of personal expenditure in daily practice (Kaplan & Berman, 2010). Dedication to the greatest organizational asset is the human resource for creating sustainable personal responsibility within the organization (Arnold, 2010, p. 75).

Personal responsibility for physiological awareness in professional performance establishes cornerstone theory, which organizational structure and strategy ultimately rely upon. Theories evolve from identifying core involvement strategies so employees meet organizational needs to organizational needs providing a framework that people work within to complete tasks. The application of self-awareness training increases participatory identification of interpersonal relational patterns and personal homeostasis within situational stress (Zender & Olshansky, 2012). The relevance of physiological research for organizational efficiency uncovers cross-disciplinary evidence of trainable physiological management with potential organizational impact. Training physiological awareness incorporates emotional self-tracking while personnel abide and influence organizational development through the presiding culture (Arnold, 2010). Organizational members create physiological reactions to emotional fluctuations throughout the duty day and often without direct, purposeful intent. Duty performance assimilates emotion for efficiency; development of emotional intelligence or a visceral knowing is an essential management talent (Awadzi Calloway, 2010; Sznycer, 2010; Tucker, 2011).

The enhancement of a collaborative shift in organizational consciousness manifests from the leadership and talent positioned toward efficiency (Pees, Shoop & Ziegenfuss, 2009). There is a common denominator developed by the sections below, a personnel baseline – both recognizable and trainable – influences from an organizational consciousness (Arnold, 2010, p. 63). Practitioner and scholarly works produce sophisticated leverage, analysis regarding human resiliency in change using relevant steps prompt a baseline adaptation for the organization in change. Relevant research in organizational efficiency identifies research topics that substantiate significant evidence of contributory personnel development with organizational initiative. Personnel development and cross-training opportunities include technology, social interactivity, lateral growth for current hierarchical structures, personal accountability, and job overlap. Continued assimilation of vast knowledge in current research formulates longevity within standards of excellence (Sharma & Talwar,

2007), including organizational consciousness. The body holds a separate and unique consciousness from the mind and is positioned to challenge the mind both in action and as a relevant aspect of reliable, functional intelligence.

Visceral Management

Physiological management involves lymph – the expansive white blood system intricately involved with neural matter, fascia, and the pervasive peripheral and central nervous systems. This involvement contributes to fatigue and pain as well as influences on both decay and preservation subject to homeostatic environmental interpretation (Sadri, 2008). Evidence suggests this interpretation contributes to an intuitive knowledge that is both consistent and reliable (McNaught, 2012). Leadership stories prevail of undocumented personal engagements reflected as "my gut told me," while documented versions provide a substantial alternate, more easily explained, and logical decision-making processes. Acknowledgment of a physiological cue in leadership or emergency performance is reflected in the use of the descriptive term visceral, adapted from the anatomical organ lining. Relational patterning and personal homeostasis are essential to the development of the topic of lymphatic management.

Lymph – Body Water

Body water permeates the soft tissues of muscle, tendon, and ligament; surrounding the nerve pathways, it roots within both blood systems (white and red) vessels. The white blood system, the lymph, protects against environmental stress and is more pervasive than the red blood system. Most people have grown familiar with their red blood system after a skinned-knee experience. The past one hundred and twenty years (note: thirty years at this point) have experienced a sharp void in public awareness of the white blood system and the many properties offered to clarify the vast potential within. Anonymous and candid interviews with medical doctors validate the sheer exoneration of this significant system from medical school studies. Instead, the lymph system was referred to as the dump or trash disposal of the human body in older medical school texts, with positive attributes rarely identified aside from the benefit of immune support. The research and dedicated years of academic practitioners bring an understanding of how the white blood system provides immunology beyond current measures and to the point of conscious control (Juhan, 1998). Injury and perceived threat exert levels of physiological demand, leaving decision-making less efficient and the person less likely to be trusted as self-accountable.

Organizational trust within personnel ranks enhances self-efficacy and personal inspiration, effectively motivating people to self-regulate and stay alert to more appropriate decisions. Performance efficiency focuses on the willingness of an individual to perform (Gerhardt, 2009); one objective determines if physiological training is relevant or influential to willingness. Relevant physiological research in organizational efficiency identifies contributory lymph adaptation and the role lymph plays through the control of innumerable physiological responses. Such adaptions include cortisol, glucose, and cytokine inflammation – roles impacting far more biological dependencies than a neighboring physical or chemical reaction (VanHoose, 2011). Dedicated efforts focused on gains in both practitioner and scholarly work produce sophisticated analyses regarding human resilience and the elements of performance depletion. Physiological research provides the consolidative theory to the prominence of self-development and motivational leadership training. Performance enhancement and interference of performance together embrace theory overlap between intentions and physiology.

Visceral Performance

Decades of debate in military stress focused on corticol-inclusive responses concluding the endocrine-reliable functions indicate dependent psychological factors. Lymph is not yet established as constitutive or consequential in this research (Long, 2012), although glucose exhibits a mechanistic cap on decision-making competency (Beedie & Lane, 2012; Gailliot & Baumeister, 2007). Perceived social-evaluative threat also creates physiological cytokine inflammation to hinder assimilation of new information in favor of personal protection (Dickerson, Gable, Irwin, et. al, 2009; Tullett, Teper & Inzlicht, 2011). And the heart, with prominent lymphatic feed, presents with an affinity to precognition (Bem, 2011). Further development of the questions regarding the lymphatic role includes recovery from ego-depletion (Inzlicht & Schmeichel, 2012; DeWall, Baumeister, Gailliot & Maner, 2008) and self-efficacy (Awadzi Calloway, 2010). The intelligent body's (Hyland, 2002) realistic potential and neuroplasticity for continual adaptability (Vance, Roberson, McGuinness, & Fazeli, 2010) provide substantial positive evidence for analysis.

Prompting human body resiliency has been established by assimilating flexible thinking (Phillips, 2011), while the risk increases when change is implemented without cognitive readiness (Fautua & Schatz, 2012). The expectation of adaptability to change becomes a social construct within groupthink; a social construct in decision-making collaborates information from both social and biological impulses. One example of a collaborative biological impulse is the mirror neuron theory, leading scientific research unintentionally toward perception presenting as objective reality, not environment (Jaffe, 2007). The impact of personal awareness, or lack of awareness, holds greater significance when considering the impact of objectivity influenced in biological collaboration. If expectation rules practice, then impression management studies (Gardner & Cleavenger, 1998) have greater application on managerial interpretations based on the manager's intuitive perspective. Personal awareness contributes to the clarity of intuition, and intuitive clarity is powerful when framed within a reliable management system that is independent of reliance on one manager. It is pertinent to consider the popularity of psychology, personality, and perceived intangible aspects of leadership such as charisma (Northouse, 2010, p. 174).

Research on the use of intuitive decision-making under non-emergency conditions (Dijksterhuis & Nordgren, 2006) provides a bridge between known facts and unidentifiable information. Unidentifiable information requires trust in leadership's ability to make healthy decisions based on experience and knowledge relevant to the circumstance. Conflict arises when trusted leadership surpasses physiological barriers of efficiency and base decisions on perceived threat that is personal fear or defense and not otherwise perceivable. Discerning knowledge versus perception in decisions is not readily duplicable in research due to the severe complexity of managerial performance (Mintzberg, 2009). Assimilating personal awareness provides insight into decisiveness; identifying intuitive recognition, including innate trust or defensiveness, denotes the need for a reliable, easy-to-use reflective template.

The Impact of Thoughtfulness

Establishing practitioner-academia research relevant to the body of knowledge in management develops through thoughtful experiential and social learning as team families unfold skill realignments. The influence of social interactivity and personal interests in management studies weave relevant personal experiences into cognitive awareness through research analysis in application. Understanding the impact of experience and interest, the criteria for research selection targets well-sourced data and analysis while not exonerating the experiential. Inspirational citizens understand the value of soft tissue states in health and stress response in daily influence: Bob Hope received daily massage (Jacksen, 2012); Tony Robbins understands the value of lymph health in decision-making and performance (DuBois, 2012); and we each control voltage panels referred to as chakras. Physiological efficiency increases through purposeful movement that directly engages the lymph, including gentle bounces to engage fun at little expenditure (http://www.healingdaily.com/exercise/rebounding-for-detoxification-and-health.htm; Tony Robbins). This style of movement is not learned; it is experienced or first observed, as a speaker preparing for a presentation observes peer aptitude more earnestly after performing personally. Physiological efficiency requires immunological authority as an organizational structure produces authoritative stature; lymph is the metaphoric example of this process in decision-making.

Comparing systemic physiological responses of human disorders metaphorically to an organization's maintenance or sanitation departments is inaccurate; lymph is more than infrastructure. Human discord is managed by an immunological authority with the power to consider options, risks, benefits, and outcomes for the organization as a whole and efficient entity. With this organizational metaphor, the reader is guided to consider the immune system as an authoritative versus reactionary response, the conscious lymph with intelligent body water. Rapid strategic application of physiological awareness develops management skills by recognition of intrapersonal physiological cues. Highly reliable management periodically performs inexplicable acts as rote performance foregoes mindful decision-making, action without physiological assimilation (Gonzalez, 2008).

The Impact of Human Thoughtfulness

Research encourages looking beyond obvious organizational needs into the impact of individual perspectives on organizational thought and identity. Organizations deal with highly efficient individuals in more areas of competence than corporate America has provided intrigue to attract, and there are personal deficits to account for. This lack of business omnipotence combined with heightened physiological awareness of an individual guides cohesive accountability for personal states of being, practicing lymphatic management. Lymphatic awareness includes developing elements of mindful physiological control. Individual duty performance, cross-training familiarity options, and use of intuitive soft skills provide greater accessible protection of vulnerable thoughts. Diane DuBois said for decades, "the whole person must come to work." Soft skills present competent management of people, prioritizing tasks, and resource allocation; these skills are quickly becoming "as vital as any traditional hard skill" (Fautua & Schatz, 2012, p. 282).

Hard skills remain essential and include the application of the Rule Principle in conscious thought, which is required when cognitive learning provides precise action and thought in operational procedures. A fundamental shift to efficient organizational development serves management in training and recognition for preparatory cognitive advantage. There is no policy to erase organizational dependency on an individual's decision-making abilities (Fautua & Schatz, 2012). The present

void in current research of physiology in personal development intricately avoids a source of consciousness separate
from the conscious mind; organizations rely upon the human
resource. Recognized human resources are strikingly similar to
what authors refer to and study as the unconscious (de Vries,
Witteman, Holland & Dijksterhuis, 2010) or the intuitive
element (McNaught, 2012). This element is available for the
reader at will.

CHAPTER FOUR
LITERATURE REVIEW CONCLUSION

The ability to duplicate research procedures suggesting a conscious link requires utilizing comprehensive, simple systematic strategies as data collection processes coded from common human perspectives. Recommendation for continued assimilation of the vast knowledge gained in current research. The body of knowledge is formulated along with excellence standards from brilliantly insightful historical minds followed for millennia (Sharma & Talwar, 2007). Together, brilliant minds honor insights from the past and validation from present research in action. Personnel engagement enriches the process and increases the likelihood of a working hypothesis in organizational dependency on personal and occupational human potential. Literature deficiencies (Creswell, 2009, Ch. 5) allow evidence for a physiologically trainable body conscience limited to conceptual and cultural miscommunication to this point (Pees, Shoop & Ziegenfuss, 2009). Resources include participants with a neutral stance on consciousness strikingly similar to the consistently reliable unconscious used in decision-making (de Vries, Witteman, Holland & Dijksterhuis, 2010) or the intuitive element (McNaught, 2012). Research efforts suggesting a conscious link require comprehensive strategies as simple, systematic, and easily understood data collection processes coded from perspective. There is a risk to performance when organizational operations develop from one person dependent on a limited scope of practice manipulated by occupational variance to another of neither. A collaborative shift in organizational consciousness toward efficiency (Pees, Shoop & Ziegenfuss, 2009) encourages looking through and beyond obvious organizational needs limited by structure.

Research requires rigorous preparation, organization, detailed descriptions, and coding to ensure "multiple strategies of validity" (Creswell, 2009, p. 177). Organizational development continues to evolve in meeting marketplace needs replicable for optimum organizational efficiencies in human resource management. The many challenges organizations face in technology and facility maintenance introduce change intervention goals that are manageable through full collaborative personnel efforts. The trends in current global markets include electronic records, stabilizing professional and client relationships (p. 653), reliance on philanthropy, consumer-directed healthcare, Baby-Boomer and Millennial populations and management (p. 654), social technology and quality regulation initiatives (p. 655). The educational trends: industrial-age roots, change, reform, models (pp. 659-664) also impact daily interventions approaching change faster and for greater lengths of time.

Manage Lymphatically

Management occurs and succeeds through action while plans loom in the near and distant futures of simultaneity in change demand. Completion of a change intervention relies upon a common language for stakeholders performing duties, the clients and communities served, and the whole of professional occupations. Due diligence is insufficient while the fields of healthcare and education perform vast feats of change, requiring micro-scale operations to be performed with competitive equipment and resource management tools. Developed software programs and portable technologies such as smartphone and laptop units have made large contributions to the industry's on-site activities while compliance care is slower in transition. The professional sector is under tremendous pressure. Adaptation is the new workplace goal requiring respect for self and others, equipment, policies, and regulatory demands while industries go forward with the competence of today's organizational staffing.

Efficient management and leadership direction for theoretical applications create a sustainable culture of organizational influence through personal responsibility (Arnold, 2010, p. 75). Many popular fields of organizational development have impact on, are impacted by, and dedicate strategies to, enhancing awareness. The fields of study in this arena include elementally specific physiological or psychological performance reactions to stress (Long, 2012). Relational impact (Zender & Olshansky, 2012) with emerging intelligence for both emotion (Johnson, 2011) and the body (Hyland, 2002) enhance organizational reliance upon an efficient human resource that has not been fully appreciated. As one employee exceeds high standards and another, fully competent, visually recedes from goals, we see that more is required than payroll and benefits for continued performance.

Performance

Interest in performance enhancement or discord and motivational success measures lead roles in whether change intervention takes root. Theoretical foundations for physiological management focus on exceptional duty performance to the detriment of focused physiologically assimilated behaviors under stress (Gonzalez, 2008). Specific strengths needed to assimilate chronic or stressful change include the ability to recognize rapid recovery opportunities for self-preservation. Resilience is critical to sustainability; understanding consciousness in continuous development includes self-awareness, which taxes the brain yet develops higher behavior function and situational awareness (Batorski, 2012). Following the nurture of a critical organizational environment and culture teaches that the essence of leadership may not be a learnable trait (Collins, 2001), while awareness is a learnable trait. The primary asset of managers is to create efficiency value through a sustainable personal responsibility culture (Arnold, 2010, p. 75). Establishing a culture focused on the use of organizational identity and task familiarity for personnel relates to deeper conceptual studies in organizational trust.

Integrity, power and influence, and justice/fairness require trust for substantive change (Horn, 2012). Long-term organizational development improvements empower participative personnel pursuits and personnel engagement by personal investment (Holman, Devane, & Cady (eds.), 2007, pp. 452) (Cooper & Markus, 1995). Discord within the realms listed above holds personnel accountable and increases recognition of another's positive responsibility as each logistically optimizes daily duty performance. Management is reliant upon data that is not readily duplicable in research efforts due to the severe complexity of management performance under specialized demand (Mintzberg, 2009). Results through decades of expert experience indicate dependence on psychological factors, whereas lymph has not been established as constitutive or consequential (Long, 2012). Physiological and lymphatic influence, your intelligent body water, weighs heartily on performance.

The global market demands competitive performance levels in civilian, civic, and military environments. Encouraging innovation in product, service, and human experientialism, current organizational operations remain fear-based and physiologically damaging. Fear-based personnel motivation encompasses culturally embraced occupational threats: a missed bonus, an evaluation on record, or a reprimand on behavior. Positive motivations also retract productivity, a reward that will set the hard-working recipient apart from peers with subtle social pressures. Each occurrence represents a common practice that disrupts fluid productivity and poses a threat to organizational positioning through resistance on minute levels that make up the whole. Research begins to understand the physiological effects of personnel resistance without the proposed solution: build awareness saturation and provide relevant training access. Collaborative cross-disciplinary success in today's workplace contributes to physiological factors aligned with a management practitioner's growing body of knowledge. Thorough academic efforts that conceive exponential developments in the optimization of organizational efficiency require the inclusion of the physiological model training that best fits the people.

Intuitive Responsibility

Reverting to old patterns of behavior remains a comfortable risk within an organization, and the characteristics will vary until change permeates systemic processes. Actions must be taken upon the shoulders of authorities accountable with absolute inclusion of the "social dimension of decision making" (Frame, 2013). The normalization of physiological interventions relies upon harmonized decision-making making, which is subject to both human capability and the "time span of discretion" (Ch. 6). Organizational participation is capable yet limited specifically to performance objectives, while the invaluability of one employee is not able to be measured due to soft skills and physiologic management. Specifically, employees hold fluid input to how best to understand award versus assessment, orient to and gain informed commitments from senior leadership, and best use of "single, integrated assessment team(s)" (Assessing a small organization, 2006). Upon assessment, the primary focuses for teams and the human resource are in the significant areas of consideration of planning and resource management (Organizational assessment, 2013).

A multitude of behavioral motivations and creatively inspiring indoctrination are available for performance enhancement of each team member based on individual skills, the intuitive included. Over the years, activities have offered and monitored simple philosophies of self-awareness and responsibility, which hold core precedents throughout organizational culture. Optimum productivity utilizes management excellence for creditable increases in organizational productivity; a strong advantage remains in developing harmonious management processes. Mintzberg (2009) addresses the dichotomy for managers who gather data, becoming both the power and demand bestowed on the manager. Specifically, the manager collects insight into avenues of decision-making from one echelon or external entity and understands or intuits the impact of effectual and ineffectual managerial leaders. Management is the match of an ambitious professional with the unrelenting task of improving efficiency and continually developing personal effectiveness for intervening in and managing change.

Five steps for sustainable momentum of change intervention in order to stay the designated course include "providing resources for change; …building a support system for change agents; …developing new competencies and skills; …reinforcing new behaviors; …(and) patience" (Cummings & Worley, 2009, pp. 180-184). Socialization tracks the focus and evolution of implementing the active promotion of a commitment from departments reliant upon this social aspect. Commitment provides vertical multi-organizational longevity with options such as reward allocation assisting the adoption of new behaviors when reinforced reliably. Reliable diffusion then ensures change efforts transfer inter-systemically with intra-systemic recognition of reliable intuitive versus data-based success. Final recognition of deviation with calibrated corrective actions produces further consistency (pp. 205-206).

CHAPTER FIVE

MIDDLE MANAGEMENT

Middle management, as the term describes, bridges founding and launching organizational goals to the daily operations and people moving these goals toward success. The manager further analyzes self-influence through exaggeration or submission of ego relative to the level of resulting success. Controversy on what makes great managers great is conversationally minimized to an "it"; what is not as obvious is the long-term analysis. Managers who present "it" and ultimately provide only charisma and certified achievements do not promote success principles of longevity. One small and highly influential element of organizational success is the tangible application of self: personnel integrate self along with the task requirements – what, when, how, who. Another element of success is the integration of self into decision-making processes and enhanced awareness of self in relation to others; helpfully, there exists a physiological barometer.

Individuals have control of personal choices and personal responses to the fluctuating states of mind and body, although some are better at self-management than others (Shaffer & Postlethwaite, 2012). Middle management became the population of interest for researching the impact on organizational efficiency, and the sample has been introduced to physiological awareness and management training. Middle management is the chosen population due to evidence that physiological management is already reliably used for organizational management, although there is limited depth in research specific to decision-making teachability. The ability to capture this skill is evasive to observation aside from using terms like intuition, intelligence, or a visceral "gut" feeling to address opportunities and obstacles. Middle managers continually address organizational needs with unique decision-making processes through rapid-fire assessment of circumstances, developing suitable adaption skills. The key concepts of physiological tools for building self-awareness begin with recognizing physiological cues such as a gut or strong feeling and 'visceral' knowledge (Vance, Roberson, McGuinness & Fazeli, 2010). Self-preservation is a natural state enhanced through increased situational awareness in an environment where threat and collaboration are clearly identifiable, leading to greater clarity (Batorski, 2012).

My original Research Proposal focused on middle managers. Middle managers strategically navigate the moving parts of complex organizational efficiency. Pilot proposals initially resulted in inconclusive data and required my initial set of questions to be revised. Based on the pilot evolution, qualitative data collected on decision-making skills include a visceral gut feeling that provides a clear mesentery message, influencing the decision yet to be made as a physiological factor. Initial focus on anatomical function for greater physiological understanding is a reliable project based upon research terms such as ego-depletion and self-efficacy (Lubbers, 2003). Current research supports this teach-ability with the body to recognize rapid recovery techniques for personnel and provide the tools for immediate recovery from perceived workplace threats. Physiological skills development is a topic of interest in management challenges today, leading toward greater organizational understanding (Campbell & Campbell, 2009).

Organizational efficiency

High-level decision-making processes feed on physical memory, creating autonomously trained physiologically efficient patterns prepared to react with consciously devised responses. Providing conceptual tools for managing workplace resilience includes identifying fear as an inefficient tool that develops reactive physiological awareness and inconsistent self-resilience (Kesting, Smolinski, & Speakman, 2010). Expertise and personnel strengths aligned with fear create management challenges based on the intrapersonal inhibitors which include the inability to gain traction in communications (Block, 2011, p. 49). The humanistic adoption of personal expression provides stabilization along the path of organizational efficiency with long-term investment returns in health and employee engagement. Physiological implications hold direct impact on the efficiency of an organization based upon environmental factors and job performance is enhanced when the whole person comes to work (Vul, Harris, Winkielman & Pashler, 2009).

MMR Methodology Introduction

Data collection tools are based on previous work by Beaudin (1983). Prior to determining organizational needs, the consultant is responsible for clarifying roles, expectations, and engaging client communications in order to receive in return the client's expectations (Block, 2006, Ch. 2). Professional perspectives challenge effective consulting with image discrepancy when even the best professional intentions for a solid proposal are presented to clients. Image discrepancy may be role- or character-based, and the costs of discrepancy include productivity and emotional (Vough, Cardador, et al., 2013). Paying close attention to detail and following lessons learned from consulting experts provide ample evidence to suggest the focus must remain on the relationship (Block, 2006, Ch. 10).

The primary asset of human resource is where change management rightly creates change value through a sustainable personal responsibility culture (Arnold, 2010, p. 75). Establishing a culture focused on the use of organizational identity and task familiarity for personnel relates to deeper conceptual studies in organizational trust. Integrity, power and influence, justice/fairness, and change management presented in MGMT 805 coursework require trust for substantive change (Horn, 2012). Discord within the realms listed above holds personal responsibility and accountability. Ease is then recognition of another's positive responsibility, as each logistically optimizes daily duty performance.

Dissertation clarifications developed from unexpected sources, as discovered when a program presenter took time to discuss strategy leading into middle management as a population of interest. Middle management within city municipal ranks will engage a dozen personnel in charge of departments versus looking at only one department. Municipal systems mimic the familiar military rank and file or traditional business models evolving under civil and social influence into lateral engagements with stakeholders, including the community. The community system here in the author's city has little public participation. In one public school meeting to discuss an Elementary teacher's dismissal, to which there was heated debate, only four community members showed. The municipal functions have a greater civic response, and one example is my city's public survey for residents. The elements of leverage are best developed under middle management based on the symposium exercises in relation to this author's topic of decision-making relevance in the sub-fields of ego depletion and resilience.

Workforce development and cross-training opportunities include technology, social interactivity, lateral growth for currently hierarchical structures, and personal accountability. Another strategically devised objective to be planned logistically and pursued diligently is the capacity for lateral growth with equal input on operations and spending. The third design is for a model week or month, one specific goal for one established period of time with no commitment of continuance. The process design maps processes and will target one segmented organizational process to template a more ambitious redesign endeavor. Finally, the one-location pilot test focuses on one clearly defined organizational location of interest (p. 458).

1. The Rapid Results Approach (RRA) employs a change sponsor, team, and facilitator with written expectations for team consistency. Specific outcomes are identified, and teams remain adaptably focused on these results. RRA works for many reasons, including the initiation of this result-focused action with little investment in pure preparation. Actions are identified as low-risk and implemented to test large-scale change. The capacity to implement action takes a stronghold with participant confidence due to the anticipation of immediacy through organizational grassroots efforts. The low risk is divided between organizational hierarchical titles, accountability throughout non-management positions, and providing personal accountability to manageable change. Further, the success of RRA includes a design intended to be replicated; there is freedom for experimentation and participants under-

stand working out the kinks of the expectations benefits all (pp. 458-460).

OD principles align with RRA philosophies to ignite and inspire, welcome eclectic passions and creativity, team-centered fun, and boldly drive human capital resource agendas (Wade, 2008). Stability is the starting asset in RRA creative action, allowing optimization of human capital investment. Leveraging organizational stability with tangible results reinforces the value of this RRA design and the five corresponding models of transparent, transformational change potentials. Guiding RRA principles focus on transformational change, with the goal of a distinctly short-term timeframe clarifying pinpointed accountability and results. RRA adoption drives change teams to experiment and discover in a disciplined environment intent on learning throughout a process of refining the next method of RRA and designing a scale-up project (Holman, Devane, & Cady (eds.), 2007, p. 457).

2. Okuno's Five Technique Model

The formation and use of a pipeline communications process where information is disseminated in part to all networked parties is another success factor of change modelling (Kaiser, 2007). Along with thoroughly intricate pipeline communications, implementable operational chains create continuity (Kabacoff, 2008), standardizing equipment and assessments create commonality (p. 369). The theoretical foundations of change preparedness require direct communication, and the model of Toshio Okuno is helpful (Cooper & Markus, 1995). Similar to the working theories of many occupational sets, Okuno's model places emphasis on a young workforce subject to heavily established status quo developed over hundreds of years.

The extensive human-level organizational dependencies of this depth in status quo require the identification of influential cross-cut variables (Feldman, 2004) optimizing empirical and theoretical approaches (Sutton, 1995). Current learning organizational environments incorporate cross-training and data or report analysis, instilling confidence within personnel ranks and effectively motivating through inspirational self-efficacy.

Self-efficacy is also a manifestation of consciousness through the body; it requires respect and expression or becomes diseased and has a direct toll on the organizational structure. Edmondson & McManus (2007) provide a matching system for data collection methodology with theory maturation, and the following chart provides baseline data collection design. Utilizing a broad template with a capacity for depth and specificity compliments transformational study efforts through personnel empowerment introduction. Preparing for change intervention based on Okuno's model incorporates the factors above through a series of workshops and practices designed for all organizational levels. Employee engagement is essential to undergo change intervention in order to best identify the direction and goals for change, encouraging the social dimension of organizational operations (Frame, 2013). RRA is built solidly upon action, as described earlier; change is irrelevant without action, and action innately contains risk subject to human protections and ethical standards.

The chart below describes actions taken as the Five Techniques and personnel targeted for each action as well as the similar change tectonics and change tactics:

Table 1 How Okuno's Five Techniques Balance Change Targets, Tectonics, and Tactics

Technique	Change Targets	Change Tectonics	Change Tactics
Group leader meetings	Manager	Incremental	• Incremental change through feedback and reinforcement • Change through insight and cognitive redefinition
Price control system	Manager	Intermediate/ revolutionary	• Parallel learning structure • Unfreezing through technological seduction
Tatsumaki program	Manager and contributor	Revolutionary	• Coercive persuasion • Explosion of myth • Parallel learning structure
Draft system	Contributor	Intermediate	• Unfreezing through technological seduction • Change through insight and cognitive redefinition • Promotion of "hybrids" (insiders with special knowledge)
Hangen game	Contributor	Revolutionary	• Explosion of myth • Parallel learning structure

Illustration courtesy of Cooper & Markus, 1995.

CHAPTER SIX

PHYSIOLOGICAL MANAGEMENT

This author believes every human uniquely interprets body water for physiological performance and enlightened decision-making. There is no point of reference from one person to another until experiential knowledge is shared and a situation is comprehensible, then serves as a point of reference for relating to connecting material. This is one area of assumption the author has naturally succeeded at reaching consensus one-on-one or in small groups, bringing the concept of lymph recognition to the participant's mind. A lot of analysis is required for this approach to succeed through integration of facial and body language, tone of voice, and receptive active listening; these interactions become intense. Self-disclosure bridges the mental conditioning of participants to word association and breaks reactions.

The reason to break personal reactive listening and response mechanisms is that baseline communications are required for the simplest concepts to be truly shared. Behavioral expression becomes visual, audible, and physically encouraging, or discouraging, and communication recipients now understand the difference in the honorable assessment of decision-making processes. This opens another discipline of research to be left alone at this time: understanding misinterpretation between similar people (culture, location, interest association, family) or close allies. Creswell recommends the use of "multiple strategies of validity," requiring rigorous preparation, organization, detailed descriptions, and coding (2009, p. 177). Organizational development continues to evolve in meeting marketplace needs replicable for optimum organizational efficiencies in human resource management.

The many challenges organizations face in technology and facility maintenance introduce change intervention goals that are manageable through full collaborative personnel efforts. The trends in current global markets include electronic records; stabilizing professional and client relationships (p. 653); reliance on philanthropy; consumer-directed healthcare; Baby-Boomer and Millennial populations and management (p. 654); social technology; and quality regulation initiatives (p. 655).

The educational trends: industrial-age roots; change; reform; models (pp. 659-664) also impact daily interventions approaching change faster and for greater lengths of time. Change interventions occur and succeed through action while plans loom in the near and distant futures of simultaneity in change demand. Completion of a change intervention relies upon a common language for stakeholders performing duties, the clients and communities served, and the whole of professional occupations.

Due diligence is insufficient while the fields of healthcare and education perform vast feats of change, requiring micro-scale operations to perform with competitive equipment and resource management tools. Developed software programs and portable technologies such as smartphone and laptop units made large contributions to the industry activities on-site while care compliance is slower in transition. Professional sectors are under pressure to perform in need of financial backing for simple shelter needs. Through mentorship and classic theory, a cross-disciplinary research model performs elemental illumination of human currencies and the ability to manage ranges of physiological health. Adaptation is the new workplace goal requiring respect for self and others, equipment, policies, and regulatory demands while the industry moves forward, gaining competence in training endeavors for today's organizational staffing.

Implementing Action Steps

Ethics in human subject research made a significant impact in the last century and developed international procedures for ensuring people as research subjects are provided full disclosure regarding risks and benefits. Creation of the Belmont Report, Declaration of Helsinki, IRBs, and the Common Rule all provide research standard frameworks: 45 Code, 21 CFR 50, and International Conference on Harmonization, to name a few, which require diligence, oversight, and transparency of intent with protection of human and personal information (http://www.hhs.gov/ohrp/index.html). The U.S. Department of Health and Human Services provides an Office for Human Research Protections to provide protection for research subjects. Additional information in the form of educational videos and webinars, community forums, quality assessment resources, and speaking opportunities are all available. There is an IRB guide available online at www.hhs.gov/ohrp/archive/irb/irb_guidebook.htm for our cohort efforts in obtaining management-relevant information through proposed data collection efforts.

The research design is non-experimental, a cross-sectional, single-stage survey, and pocket graph data collection tool.

Supervised under the direction of a mentor/instructor based on voluntary participation after appropriate authorization, a precursor to launching an expansive project after analysis. Exploring physiological processes begins with a simple survey to evaluate personnel participation and the relevance of individual awareness and resiliency skills. Evaluation and peer debriefing of data is essential; social construct is reliant upon the most accurate collaborative information subject to influence social or biological impact. This author is interested in a methodologically simplistic effort providing distinct baseline commonality from the multitude of forms of organizational indoctrination available.

Indoctrination becomes a tool for optimum productive capability utilized in organizational excellence. Creditable or corrective management increases organizational productivity through individualizing optimum physiological efficiency based on data analysis relative to work. Immediate goals include utilizing as simple a format as possible for gathering data through concurrent, transformational, and quantitative formats. Embedded qualitative data is gathered through digital surveys and data collection cards. SurveyMonkey is utilized to sustain the survey integrity and provide an electronic survey completion notification identifiable by two random and anonymous coding procedures. Responses predict the validity of this collection strategy and obtain concurrent information regarding the validity of correlated variables reliant upon organizational and developmental experience. The simple electronic survey also constructs items for measuring the hypothetical variables and conceptual correlation regarding physiological awareness through developmental experience. Data capture is relatively simple, although the voluntary participants provide results that indicate evaluative adjustments needed to the design strategy, which are cost-effective and convenient. The free survey tools that provide room for evaluation and continual improvement are a beginning step. The main quantitative data collection instrument is a simple 6x4 sheet of printer paper with a graph that inquires participants to identify tangible and professional soft skills. The quantitative portion of the electronic survey is complete with demographics or yes/no responses; each question allows feedback.

There are reflection and expanded qualitative data windows for brief or detailed open-ended explanations of the quantitative answer provided. Inductive data analysis developed this theoretical strategy through personal accounts and multitudes of research reviews not to be confused with epistemology or ontology. Qualitative aspects guide an unfolding path toward further potential that is not reliant upon the central question. Directors will be provided coded surveys to be taken online as explained in the letter of consent and provided the opportunity to record expectations ahead of time. The number of participants is anticipated to be twelve, the current number of departments.

Additional Informed Consent is provided through the survey's first question and consent statement; all collected data will be documented and saved for seven years at the researcher this author's office. The incentive at this time is a sense of contribution to personal care and minimizing occupational stress. It will be stated that the employee is not to talk openly about answers to questions or offer or solicit opinions regarding the survey or a specific question. The employee places themself and others at risk for invalid data when discussing anonymous concepts, jeopardizing confidentiality and, ultimately, the potential for legitimate creative insights. The letter states not to discuss any portion of the survey to include whether one participated or not with organizational personnel.

The smallest amount of information may be enough to identify a participant. The initial survey process will collect minimal demographics and no work history until the researcher is certain that project ethics are understood and applied competently during this learning phase. There is limited perceived Conflict of Interest. Participants engaged survey options with no distress. My approach to welcoming subjective data also resulted in more than one creative short story. One participant anonymously paragraphed his respectful, joyful, and purposeful cosplay. The research continued.

CHAPTER SEVEN

RESEARCH METHODOLOGY INTRODUCTION

Baldrige assessment tips are revisited for staying on track with the management consult, including assessment prior to deciding need; understanding award versus assessment; orienting and gaining informed commitment from senior leadership; and an integrated assessment team per operational segment (Assessing a small organization, 2006). Through the use of available resources and instructor guidance with peer responses, this project will get off to a smooth start and provide assistance in both this author's academic endeavor and municipal development.

Sample Contract Elements

Purpose of the Study

The purpose of this study is for the consultant to assist department directors in gaining familiarity with a municipal learning organization as determined relative to the organization. The main goal is to identify personnel performance efficiency standards in preparation for organizational change intervention. An additional benefit is this research provides str re-set practices for managing central nervous stress assimilation through change implementation.

Participants

All municipal department directors are encouraged to participate in the study for insight into organizational impacts on stress management in the workplace.

Procedures

Volunteers will participate in this study by doing the following: 1) completing an informed consent form, 2) answering specific questions through a MonkeySurvey link in regard to the workplace demand and impact, 3) donate donating approximately one (1) hour of weekly meeting time through the next four weeks.

Benefits of Participation

Participants in this study should recognize gain by applying simple techniques for managing resilience.

Risks of Participation

There are risks involved in all research studies. This study is estimated to involve low risk to the participants. However, it is natural for participants to have feelings when answering questions of uncomfortableness or perhaps a feeling of retribution if negative comments are made regarding the organization in this survey. All participant input remains anonymous, and identifying documents (this form) are secured.

_______________End of sample contract____________

This author had previously established soft tissue recovery consultation with middle management for a greater understanding of the human element within their specific workforce. A director's benefits include quantifiable results from points in any day when decision-making was engaged or hindered and whether focused inward attention turns a dilemma into the optimal decision. Further benefits include awareness of oneself and workplace resiliency. As with most endeavors, the greater investment and honesty volunteers offer, the greater will be their results. Paying attention to physiological decision-making patterns brings each manager into a reflective position based on self-awareness first, then based on interpersonal influence.

Audience

The initial target research audience was limited to volunteer director participants for municipal departments and state-run facilities for mental stabilization. This proposal moved beyond the audience and into the systems. Management and organizational decision-makers at any level of responsibility are the ultimate target population. Interest remains in the human resource, including and beyond short project durations. This research continues to evolve, as does the individual of any organized structure reliant on performance. Overall success measures that are not quantitatively consistent will develop; this includes an audience complex yet limited organizationally by a unit such as families with individual characteristics regardless of the family size. Characteristics in self-regulation, motivation, organizational logistics, and a few life experiences contribute to an intriguing body of knowledge. The immediate audience includes this author, course instructor, the course instructor, the participating organization, and professional colleagues. The project audience ultimately becomes employees to leaders from any occupationally specific realm.

In an article dated June 20, 2017, Hannah Brockhaus quotes Pope Francis on the education of young people. "There are so many things to be taught, ... but the essential thing is the growth of a free conscience, capable of confronting itself with reality and of orienting itself in (reality) guided by love, by the desire to compromise with others, to take on the weight of their difficulties and wounds, to escape from all selfishness to serve the common good." *(Retrieved on June 20, 2017, from https://cruxnow.com/vatican/2017/06/20/responsibility-seek-truth-educate-youth-pope-francis-says/)*

The initial sample began a collection of data through a professional audience in Cohort 33 with ample life and organizational experience. Cohort 33 folks were interested in contributing; each provided initial clarification efforts as this sample constitutes diversity from successful professional backgrounds. Combine this with unique levels of personal awareness regarding the ability to identify physiological management in leadership increasing greater, increasing the potential for relevant data. Additional projects with similar intent have been conducted with military exercises, both in Garrison and field training. Prior to exposure to academic requirements, this data was gathered by the policies in place. After each training, event, or demonstration, participants hold an AAR, After Action Review. During these brief, though not rushed, meetings, all participants are encouraged to provide input for three reflections: 1. What went well? 2. What requires improvement? 3. What can we do better next time?

Decades of After Action Reviews result in a conclusive, comprehensive baseline: respect.

Current Design Features

[Include links to theory and all relevant areas]

Engaging realistic expectations in return for honest and direct procedural input from the consultant, one municipality evolved the Open Systems Theory (Ch. 22). A municipal system's impact on the real world is immediate. In preparation for working with the ...'s department directors, steps are needed to best understand the city's responsibilities. Implications of organizational theory for change managers produce perceived irreplaceable experiences and create protocol on what is later determined as a personality trait by previous leadership. Governance is a system that provides a secondary structure in order to best observe beyond daily sectors of responsibility (Galbraith, Downey, & Kates, 2002, Ch. 3). Galbraith, Downey & Kates, 2002 – skepticism is not fear, avoidance of the mess in getting there (p. 261). Confronting thought processes that previous efforts were incorrect means more work and power is threatened (p. 263). Satisficing due to rapid change need dilutes deep/critical thinking (LC, 5/4/14, pulled 5/12/2014).

Processes [time, resources, actions, and models]

Prior to determining organizational needs, the consultant is responsible for clarifying role expectations and engaging client communications in order to confirm the client's expectations (Block, 2006, Ch. 2). Professional perspectives challenge effective consulting with image discrepancy when even the best professional intentions for a solid proposal are presented to clients. Image discrepancy may be role- or character-based, and the costs of discrepancy include productivity and emotional (Vough, Cardador et al., 2013). Paying close attention to detail and following lessons learned from consulting experts provide ample evidence to suggest the focus must remain on the relationship (Block, 2006, Ch. 10). The primary asset of human resource is where change management rightly creates change value through a sustainable personal responsibility culture (Arnold, 2010, p. 75). Discord within organizational trust holds personal responsibility accountable, and recognition of another's positive responsibility, as each logistically optimizes daily duty performance.

My doctoral University's Spring Symposium provided opportunities for dissertation clarification from unexpected sources, as discovered when a program presenter had time to discuss and question my mid-point progress. Targeting mid-management in the city municipal ranks will engage only a few personnel in charge of departments versus looking at only one department. Municipal systems mimic the familiar military rank and file or traditional business models evolving under civil and social influence into lateral engagements with stakeholders, including the community. The community system here in the author's city has heated debate. Municipal functions hold great civic impact, and our the city underwent a city-wide survey for residents to assist.

Leveraging Knowledge

Continued assimilation of vast knowledge in current research formulates longevity within standards of excellence (Sharma & Talwar, 2007), including organizational consciousness. The body holds separate and unique consciousness from the mind; body consciousness is positioned to challenge the mind both in action and as a relevant aspect of reliable, functional intelligence. Organizationally competitive statures of today encourage personnel as the change intervention reinforces transparency, an increasingly common organizational practice in today's business culture. A transformational study between behavior and personal awareness explored with RRA or OFT still offers the opportunity to mix data methods, allowing participants to expand or specify perspectives. The reason for combining both quantitative and qualitative data is to better understand research problems through the cross-cutting of multiple variables, providing convergence. People express personal awareness in a variety of manners, including physiological responses as recognized components of chosen performance standards (Creswell, 2009, p. 123).

Pre-change implementation steps are limited in the RRA, and in the OFT, these steps encourage establishing best practices based on fundamental beliefs. One foundational belief in organizational development is that the person performing a duty knows the task inefficiencies best and is also the best individual or team to handle process management. Subjective measures are applied for relevant applications of mindfulness, and the organizational creation of acceptance for ambiguity within rapidly evolving research. Data collection methodologies present ideal mixes in format utilizing concurrent, transformational, quantitative with embedded qualitative (Creswell, 2009), and mixed co-relational (Glatthorn & Joyner, 2005) surveys. Transparency minimizes risk to participants possessing life-consciousness capable of being physiologically (and/or psychologically) or intellectually acted upon. The mind consciousness associated with complex brain matter filters actionable sensory input when communicating.

There is no doubt for this author that each research participant will have experienced a level of emotion, inspiration, intuition, or other subjective influence worthy of incorporating as organizational intuition. Every level of personnel engagement will enrich the process and increase the likelihood of a working hypothesis in organizational dependency on personal and occupational human potential. Literature deficiencies (Creswell, 2009, Ch. 5) allow evidence for a physiologically trainable body conscience limited to conceptual and cultural miscommunication to this point (Pees, Shoop & Ziegenfuss, 2009). Resources for change intervention include participants with a neutral stance on consciousness, strikingly similar to the consistently reliable unconscious used in decision-making (de Vries, Witteman, Holland & Dijksterhuis, 2010) or the intuitive element (McNaught, 2012). Research efforts suggesting a conscious link require comprehensive strategies as simple, systematic, and easily understood data collection processes coded from perspective. There is a risk to performance when the organizational culture develops from one person dependent on a limited scope of practice manipulated by occupational variance. A collaborative shift in organizational consciousness toward efficiency by Pees, Shoop & Ziegenfuss (2009) encourages looking through and beyond obvious organizational needs.

Consideration for consistent and ongoing change evaluation of RRA and OFT involves the management of revolving data to represent readily available growth charts from the perspective and experience of research participants (Creswell, 2009). A methodologically simplistic effort remains replicable, providing distinct baseline commonality from the multitude of motivational and inspirational indoctrinations available for performance enhancement. Over the years activities, activities have offered and monitored simple philosophies of self-awareness and responsibility, which hold core precedents throughout organizational culture. Optimum productivity utilizes management excellence for creditable increases in organizational productivity; a strong advantage remains in developing harmonious management processes. Mintzberg (2009) addresses the dichotomy for managers who gather data, becoming both the power and demand bestowed on the manager. Specifically, the manager collects insight into avenues of decision-making from one echelon or external entity and understands the impact of ineffectual leaders.

RRA brings to the table functional implementation without planning; planning is accomplished as an action research portion of data collection alongside result reporting. OFT establishes a framework of creativity and role play directly within the senior and mid-level management team meetings as well as front-line management and personnel work sectors. Delegating delicate information with awareness of personnel impact allows the actions expected to avoid being "performed inadequately, by the uninformed" (p. 175). A positive and balanced field of expectation regarding personal productivity, not duplicating efforts, leads to mutual respect and sustainability. Mintzberg's managerial effectiveness focuses on balance within the threads of energy, reflection, analysis, worldliness, collaboration, proactivity, and social integration; through this process, managers think for themselves while performing (Ch. 6). Mintzberg's casually rational approach to management depicts the very real conundrum of management not as an autonomous profession or as an occupation (p. 222). Management is the match of an ambitious professional with the unrelenting task of improving efficiency and continually developing personal effectiveness.

Organizational Development requires professional opinion applied from integrated knowledge and collaborative experience for new consultants. Areas of expertise are developed in consulting practice through following established intervention models and assessing organizationally specific responses or adaptations to intervention. Points of discussion include ten recommended steps involved in post-change process implementation. Methods of minimizing risk for the process include preparation for reverting to familiar behaviors and determining change implementation elements and action steps. The use of hybrid resourced materials provides a lively look into post-implementation below. Steps and elements of change involve the continuous evaluation and recognition of the human resource initiatives undergoing change through the use of post-change assessment.

The phase of assessment after the change process, has been implemented with ten steps: five relative to sustainable momentum and five for institutionalization processes. Five steps for sustainable momentum of change intervention in order to stay the designated course include "providing resources for change; ... building a support system for change agents; ... developing new competencies and skills; ... reinforcing new behaviors; ... (and) patience" (Cummings & Worley, 2009, pp. 180-184). Socialization tracks the focus and evolution of implementing active change promotion. Commitment provides vertical multi-organizational longevity with reward allocation assisting the adoption of new behaviors when reinforced consistently. Diffusion ensures change efforts transfer inter-systemically and final recognition of deviation with calibrated corrective actions produces further consistency (pp. 205-206).

Sustaining intervention characteristics are helpful in protecting and include the next five features detailed by Cummings and Worley (2009). The first two features of the next five, are to gain goal specificity and programmability within the workforce; to allow everyone transparent personal developments while implementing new cultural identity (p. 204). Further, identify at which level the change is targeted for change value; this is powerful and not to be mistaken for a wedge where efficiency was already strong (pp. 204-205). Finally, the last two features gain internal support and resourceful sponsorship. Internal and external support encourages organizational change, while sponsorship at the appropriate level in seniority encourages the allocation of resources for the decrease in change impact risk (p. 205).

The institutionalization framework engages each of the steps and elements of change by level of accountability and implementation for sustaining change efforts. Each organizational level includes characteristics in congruence, stability for organizational environment and technology, as well as organizational unionization. These three key dimensions provide oversight of the change intervention throughout the hierarchy, leading into specificity for both the characteristics and institutionalization discussed above with formal evaluation of success indicators by the what, who, and where of the organization:

1. Congruence

a. Management - intervention harmonized with "managerial philosophy, strategy, and structure" (pp. 203-204)

b. Individual - member commitment facilitates persistent personnel development

2. Environmental and Technological Stability

a. Senior Leadership - embedded into the organizational culture and design processes

b. Organization-wide vigilance at all levels - rapid change creates discord and market demand adjustment

3. Unionization

a. Workforce/Management - relationship is required

b. Collaborative efforts involved in stabilizing organizational design strategies with job enrichment (p. 204).

CHAPTER EIGHT

RESEARCH METHODOLOGY CONCLUSION

The two change processes, RRA and OFT, were chosen for their applicability to small business operations with potential for growth applications. The primary asset of human resource is where change management rightly creates change value through a sustainable personal responsibility culture (Arnold, 2010, p. 75). Establishing a culture focused on the use of organizational identity and task familiarity for personnel relates to deeper conceptual studies in organizational trust. Integrity, power and influence, and justice/fairness through change management require trust for substantive change (Horn, 2012); RRA and OFT permeate organizational trust. RRA and OFT long-term change improvements empower participative personnel pursuits; both engage personnel with personal investment (Holman, Devane, & Cady (eds.), 2007, pp. 452) (Cooper & Markus, 1995). Discord within the realms listed above holds personal responsibility accountable, and recognition of another's positive responsibility, as each logistically optimizes daily duty performance.

Municipal departments incorporate a wide range of public service; the processes, strategy, and design remain rurally pragmatic within the culture, mission, and vision. One established code and charter prompted a municipality to adopt the Home Rule IAW, the US Constitution Article XX, which keeps local problems in the hands of local residents. Opportunities are available for a project of fair scope, building upon data obtained from a city survey conducted the fall season prior to conducting this research project. In preparation for weekly director meetings, a number of inputs were gathered for analysis based on public information and data obtained through two pilot studies over the last six months. One study was conducted through a local private business with ample voice in local affairs; one study was conducted through a local government department with a previously employed director. Areas of interest in physiological training are included for analysis in change management in this paper through the star model intended for whole-system impact (Galbraith, Downey, & Kates, 2002). Star analysis is an appropriate tool to assess organizational mission alignment of Strategy, Structure, Processes, People, and a Reward System (Galbraith, Downey & Kates, 2002). Understanding the latter is important for continued research. A public copy of the municipality's reward system is not available without an interview and is addressed only briefly.

The most recent pilot research provides internal data otherwise unavailable; award versus assessment is reflected upon based on this most recent pilot collection. Care will be taken to engage participating personnel from an appreciative stance, not overly taxing performance, through the use of pocket charts. Participants will annotate progress through the use of these cards on the proposed topic of discussion, minimizing distraction from pertinent activities; this ends the discussion on known rewards. Werther (1999) states that "structure can drive strategy" (p. 13). Talent and capital each focus on value and core competencies with a virtual organization (p. 14); assumed right actions are not always optimum. Getting tunnel vision on doing right, instead of doing the right things for the organization, leads to unnecessary costs in resources (p. 15). Werther (1999) also states no value exists in sacrificing organizational responsiveness for the ease of a rigid hierarchical command and control (p. 16).

The ability to orient and gain informed commitment from senior leadership is an expectation throughout participation of volunteers as a "single, integrated assessment team" (Assessing a small organization, 2006). The targeted participation group for assessment includes future planning and resource management (Organizational assessment, 2013), requiring specialized participants. The proposed volunteer directors will discuss the practicality of a short-reference pocket reader during workday decision-making negotiations; input will be collected continually and evaluated for efficient analysis. Job enrichment is a significant factor for participating executives. Middle management routinely optimizes physiological efficiency by utilizing decision-making strategies. I conclude that my proposal is qualified and substantiated; decision-making skills may be enhanced by optimizing physiological efficiency. Let us apply inclusive diversity in change allowance for intuitive decision-making soft skills development of organizational culture and manage lymphatically.

CHAPTER NINE

PHYSIOLOGY OF PRACTICAL DECISION-MAKING

Health and wellness have grabbed organizational interest for decades. It is not this author's intent to provide practical steps for the health and wellness of organizational managers. Those recommendations are expressly provided through public video on body movement for physiological impact. These videos are the beginning of soft tissue recovery (str). The author's intent is to prove that organizations want to focus on str in order to improve decision-making skills within management's often-required, rapid-response operating field. Str is referred to a number of times throughout this dissertation research in public presentation and daily in community conversation. The introduction to str is this author's inherent interest in offering solutions. Str may not be your solution; it is one application to resolving organizational decision-making errors happening in rapid-response scenarios, which impact an individual's decision-making ability significantly both at work and personal time.

Organizational efficiency relies upon the physiological efficiency of employees and executives. The loss or rotation of trained personnel due to stressors on health and wellness creates change for those gaining operational familiarity. Although change happens on far larger scales, creating organizational stress or inefficiency, the premise of physiological considerations for organizational workforces, executives, contracts, and more centers on the premise that obvious and stress-inducing change is not the only force which management should be concerned with. Please welcome concern for the physiological processes also reliant upon decision-making efficiency within what may be considered normal responses during non-change periods.

Experienced managers discern external impact from internal organizational decisions through direct accountability of the decision-maker when available. Decisions may present as external threats beyond a mere force of doing business. Organic stress management tools embrace awareness of threat management in the decision-making framework. Creating a decision-making design to encourage input throughout stakeholders while encouraging learned and innate abilities for efficiently managing self.

Inclusive Equity in Policy

Effective management maintains professional awareness of observable behaviors while tracking outcomes for management-observed decision-making processes or evaluations. Awareness of decision-making behaviors assists in gauging employee productivity and longevity of those committed to an organization. Traditional concepts rely upon diligent workers motivated by reimbursement or similar benefits. Nontraditional concepts of working people encourage the use of organic management tools for self and team sustainability. Embrace selfless patterns to analyze the organizational impact of respect for people beyond the limitations of self and into community apart from organizational initiatives.

Personal Peer Review Request (PPRR)

We, The People, own, recover, and optimize ourselves most efficiently. Recovery is a recognized platform before we optimize much of anything we own, such as our stress responses while experiencing a major life event or a subtle change at work. Str was inevitable while facing unnerving life scenarios. Str was my refuge; I needed to recover from old injuries. I knew early into motherhood that an aggressive ope would quickly become my adult-algorithm for life. Optimizing what did work was going to be essential. Branded ten years before str, ope was this author's lighthouse. A mental daily goal, shining in any doorway or vertical opportunity to optimize a body movement for greater efficiency. These small active body goals have led to invaluable insight. I was and remain open to the glory we hold in positive potential.

Optimization was my policy, my consistent response when consciousness crowns a person to behave assertively and attentively. Decision-making, whether long-term planning or instantaneous reactivity, is a crown of consciousness enhanced through experience, exchange, and interaction. While optimizing focused areas of life, the need to discern areas of recovery remains apparent. This author is a firm believer that our greatness is magnified when great ideas are successfully passed along for the knowing. Also, I believe that our weakest parts may be challenged for improvement. Mostly, I believe in my peers' ability to think things through. Then, to take action. We're Generation X, some of US here. We do it all. I tell you, I know the most amazing folks throughout many generations.

We belong to a People of longevity. We may be young on the scale of known Ages and species, but still, we deserve to recognize ourselves. We deserve to include ourselves in our conversations. Our homeostatic balance, a healthy physiology, is another part of or another part of optimizing our personal decision-making skills. Deciding to rely upon an optimizing framework of inclusive efficiency, collection of data, and thoughtful analysis applies to all areas of life. It is not enough to be passively heard in a corporate meeting; it is enough to know with certainty that your voice and clear expression are instantaneously incorporated into all stakeholder considerations. Through exchange and interaction, I wish for this short book to prompt decision-making conversations honed toward positive potentials regardless of the topic or circumstance. Here, I request a Peer Review from my phenomenal peers.

Technology assists; it is quite helpful; still, no technology replaces you. Your organization is reliant upon you optimizing yourself and including the organization in your personal plans. Inclusion between you and your organization includes you and your decision-making optimization. Incorporating lymphatic management practices for human care, from recovery to optimization, is one conversation available for managers mindfully engaging you and your decision-making optimization. Knowing your people requires investments beyond any available reference guide. Practicing decision-making optimization in macro and micro opportunities, actively and practically, reinforces stable and secure responsiveness. Stable and secure responsiveness establishes circumstantial empowerment to enhance organizational efficiency prior to establishing changes to policy during change of any less familiar or less obvious nature. Decision-making is the focus for an inclusive and efficient response in many work environments. Decision-making is documented to rapidly wane during periods of human fatigue, injury, or illness. Stable and secure responsiveness does more for a workforce than provide the schedule. Empowerment of a consistent cultural directive, efficiently exercised into instantaneous action, is often relieving to the management or senior supervisors making too many decisions for efficient decision-making recovery.

The human condition is phenomenal. We are even more phenomenal when provided an allowance for the inclusion of the human response in decision-making. We are adaptable. We are best at adapting what we are already familiar with in order to properly adapt a new solution from known parts. One popular expression for the relief of making a reasonable decision based on known factors is the visual comment of minimizing parts of the decision that fluctuate, or "move." A straightforward opportunity with varying options is far more reliable when suggesting or directing a solution after one has "minimized the moving parts." Stable and secure, then familiar and adaptable. A leader is able to reinforce personal vulnerabilities when those who are able to do so make allowance to reinforce known vulnerabilities. It is a decision to acknowledge vulnerabilities.

Acknowledging a vulnerability is a caring move. Our vulnerabilities may be the cornerstone we build upon. We build families through sharing the vulnerabilities of home and emotion. We build careers on the vulnerabilities of someone else's dream and a vulnerable concept of reimbursement for personal investment. Decades of research are available on the homeostatic balance humans bring to other humans. I have witnessed how we naturally make up for differences and reinforce group balance. Over a matter of weeks, humans are able to sync verbal, physical, and physiological responses as well. Physiological balance, homeostasis, and immunity are instantaneously responsive to our next calendar event, to a phone call, and more broadly to a fluctuating or adjustable environment of work-home life. There is more to being human than family and work. We hold creative compassion. We care.

Our immune responses will be discussed generally throughout this research book. It is a magical system of healing within our systems. Our immune responses are dispatched to sound, contact, and even intuition; sometimes, we will recognize an approach without seeing or hearing it. Individual responses to stimuli are anticipated; we may even respond to dreams as if they are external stimuli. Similarly, one's place of work provides a cultural experience, even if an employee does not consider their work life to hold a personal influence. An organization's culture seeps into civil and private lives. The culture of work and home influences a person's decision-making skills; one may use work processes at home as a simplification to cultural discord. As one example of discordant cultural influences, you may have heard stories about a family member being too staunch, too neat, or too something after returning from military, religious, global education, or travels. Stable and secure responses encourage learned behaviors and honed decision-making skills for individuals working within one stable and securely responsive organizational culture. It is recommended to respect one's home life outside work, too.

Learned behaviors impact lymph. Lymph is one element of our human healing processes. Our lymphatic healers work gleefully along. It will flow, healing from the inside with no decision-making attention offered at all. Contrarily, we are minimizing organizational efficiency through workforce exclusion and inefficient or conflicting operating policies because our immune systems respond to such stimuli directly. Exclusion encourages physiological disruption to the flow of a healthy immune system. I learned that in third grade. It was decades later that I learned the flow of lymph during real-time navigations may become stagnant in directed negative influence. On the other hand, lymph likes the emotion of joy immensely, according to some research and volumes documented in healing journey journals.

Personal experience holds value to an organization through each stakeholder's private learning in matters of personal security or one of many other ways to express the commonality and healthy exchange of a workforce. How one person maintains their homeostasis impacts the efficiency of a team, mission, and family. How one person maintains optimum decision-making skills within an organization is behaviorally conditioned at work, impacting all stakeholders. People care about complex and comprehensive influences on one's decision-making processes because people impact people.

Sharing a quality human experience during unprecedented times is my honor. The author's academic journey has been enhanced through the use of body-read, meditation, and what the author calls her ability to read the air. The knowledge gained through these techniques is applicable. The use of these techniques is referred to as soft technology. Our human physiology also utilizes soft technology. The branding of str as a lymphatic management tool to further garner ope recognition took a fascinating turn when I realized these bodywork efforts, the mindfulness, and the specificity of data that flows from these engagements were also being used for enhancing decision-making skills. The author further recognized body markers, tell-tale signs of an environmental read through a physiological awareness, which was noticeably relied upon during times of organizational change.

Life events, organizational development and change, all the moving parts of my life, led to an ABD: All But Done, or All But Dissertation. I publish my interests in Doctoral research under the work of my academy for str and ope. I stress this material has changed my life. I share this writing because recognizing the efforts of many who become silenced has become my mission. The works of positive human potential are not new, and the body continues to heal. Reminding folks that these works of positive human potential are not new and being able to provide current, modern, academic works to prove they are also not forgotten is my mission. Reminding folks that our bodies continue to heal, generally, and being able to provide current, modern, academic works to prove this is not forgotten is also my mission.

This writing provides a few short notes for health and well-being. Most significant to my str ope causes is a solid desire to share one well-pondered tip. While you are required to make lightning-speed pronouncements, while new potentials are spiraling in your direction, mindfulness is helpful. Also helpful are routine conditions that prioritize ope during decision-making efforts required by an organization prior to any need for human recovery, or str. The following are final statements focusing on str and ope. The development of Sheri's branding ope began over thirty years ago. Development of str branding followed after realizing there are times, and places within the human body, which require us to back up and begin recovery prior to optimizing a next best move. Therefore, I publish ABD.

FINAL RECOMMENDATIONS

Be impossible. Be you. Bestow your great assertions upon yourself first; do not hesitate to shine outward throughout time, space, and frequency attentions. Move swiftly inward. Balance forward, backward, sideward, and vertically. There are tangents of potential faceting all surfaces within and beyond observation. You create as you observe, in a manner no other may create, so unique you are. Collaborate, knowing. Experientially learn your carbon potentials are exponential. Drive the ship.

The publication is an unfolding journey into one factor, ope, proven to macro-micro fluctuate in organizational activities influencing decision-making at all times while enhancing decision-making skills through proper homeostatic awareness. The value of healing and recovering one's soft tissues is true body knowledge, and the greater catalyst to optimized physiology is the emotion of joy. Our reasoning may suffer circumstance. I strongly feel strongly and listen closely to empirical data that discerns physiological responses that impact decision-making. Living freely in movement and confidently making the best decisions is not always a purposeful or consciously engaged act. Decision-making is proven to be more efficient when provided rejuvenation via sport, meditation, medical appointments, or potential lessons in self-awareness. The practical application of lymphatic management for improved decision-making skills is inclusive and collaboratively efficient; folks want it to work.

Manage Lymphatically: optimize physiological efficiency for decision-making discernment.

ADDENDUM 1

The Metaphysics of Morals
Introduction to the Theory of Right

A. Definition of the Theory of Right

The sum total of those laws which can be incorporated into external legislation is termed the theory of right (Ius). If legislation of this kind actually exists, the theory is one of positive rights. If a person who is conversant with it or has studied it (Iuriconsultus) is acquainted with the external laws in their external function, i.e., In their application to instances encountered in experience, he is said to be experienced in matters of right (Iurisperitus). This body of theory may amount to the same as jurisprudence (Iurisprudentia), but it will remain only the science of right (Iuriscientia) unless both its elements are present. The latter designation applies to a systemic knowledge of the theory of natural right (Iusnaturae), although it is the student of natural right who has to supply the immutable principles on which all positive legislation must rest.

B. What is Right?

The jurist, if he does not wish to lapse into tautology or to base his answer on the laws of a particular country at a particular time instead of offering a comprehensive solution, may well be just as perplexed on being asked this as the logician is by the notorious question: 'What is truth?' He will certainly be able to tell us what is legally right (quid sit iruis) within a given context, i.e., what the laws say or have said in a particular place and at a particular time: but whether their provisions are also in keeping with right, and whether they constitute a universal criterion by which we may recognize in general what is right and what is unjust (iustum et iniustum), are questions whose answers will remain concealed from him unless he abandons such empirical principles for a time and looks for the sources of these judgments in the realm of pure reason. This will enable him to lay the foundations of all possible legislation. And while empirical laws may give him valuable guidance, a purely empirical theory of right, like the wooden head in Phaedrus's fable, may have a fine appearance but will, unfortunately, contain no brain.

The concept of right, in so far as it is connected with a corresponding obligation (i.e., the moral concept of right), applies within the following conditions. Firstly, it applies only to those relationships between one person and another, which are both external and practical, that is, in so far as their actions can, in fact, influence each other either directly or indirectly. But secondly, it does not concern the relationship between the will of one person and the desires of another (and hence only the latter's needs, as in acts of benevolence or hardheartedness); it concerns only the relationship between the will of the first and the will of the second. And thirdly, the will's material aspect, i.e., the end which each party intends to accomplish by means of the object of his will, is completely irrelevant in this mutual relationship; for example, we need not ask whether someone who buys goods from me for his own commercial use will gain anything in the process. For we are interested only in the form of the relationship between the two wills, in so far as they are regarded as free, and in whether the action of one of the two parties can be reconciled with the freedom of the other in accordance with a universal law.

Right is, therefore, the sum total of those conditions within which the will of one person can be reconciled with the will of another in accordance with a universal law of freedom.

C. The Universal Principle of Rights

'Every action which by itself or by its maxim enables the freedom of each individual's will to co-exist with the freedom of everyone else in accordance with a universal law is right.'

Thus, if my action or my situation in general can co-exist with the freedom of everyone in accordance with a universal law, anyone who hinders me in either does me an injustice, for this hindrance or resistance cannot co-exist with freedom in accordance with universal laws.

It also follows from this that I cannot be required to make this principle of all maxims my own maxim, i.e., to make it the maxim of my own actions, for each individual can be free so long as I do not interfere with his freedom by my external actions, even although his freedom may be a matter of total indifference to me or although I may wish in my heart to deprive him of it. That I should make it my maxim to act in accordance with right is a requirement laid down for me by ethics.

Thus the universal law of right is as follows: let your external actions be such that the free application of your will can co-exist with the freedom of everyone in accordance with a universal law. And although this law imposes an obligation on me, it does not mean that I am in any way expected, far less required, to restrict my freedom myself to these conditions purely for the sake of this obligation. On the contrary, reason merely says that individual freedom is restricted in this way by virtue of the idea behind it, and that it may also be actively restricted by others; and it states this as a postulate which does not admit of any further proof.

It it is not our intention to teach virtue, but only to state what is right, we may not and should not ourselves represent this law of right as a possible motive for actions.

D. Right entails the Authority to use Coercion

Any resistance which counteracts the hindrance of an effect helps to promote this effect and is consonant with it. Now everything that is contrary to right is a hindrance to freedom based on univeral laws (i.e. if it is contrary to right), any coercion which is used against it will be a hindrance to a hindrance of freedom, and will thus be consonant with freedom in accordance with universal laws – that is, it will be right. It thus follows by the law of contradiction that right entails the authority to apply coercion to anyone who infringes it.

E. In its 'strict' Sense, Right can also be envisaged as the Possibility of a general and reciprocal Coercion consonant with the Freedom of Everyone in accordance with Universal Laws

This proposition implies that we should not conceive of right as being composed of two elements, namely the obligation imposed by a law, and the authority which someone who obligates another party through his will possesses to coerce the latter into carrying out the obligation in question. Instead, the concept of right should be seen as consisting immediately of the possibility of universal reciprocal coercion being combined with the freedom of everyone. For just as the only object of right in general is the external aspect of actions, right in its strict sense, i.e., right unmixed with any ethical considerations, requires no determinants of the will apart from purely external ones; for it will then be pure and will not be confounded with any precepts of virtue. Thus, only a completely external right can be called right in the strict (or narrow) sense. This right is certainly based on each individual's awareness of his obligations within the law; but if it is to remain pure, it may not and cannot appeal to this awareness as a motive which might determine the will to act in accordance with it, and it, therefore, depends rather on the principle of the possibility of an external coercion which can coexist with the freedom of everyone in accordance with universal laws.

Thus when it is said that a creditor has a right to require the debtor to pay his debt, it does not mean that he can make the latter feel that his reason itself obliges him to act in this way. It means instead that the use of coercion to compel everyone to do this can very well be reconciled with everyone's freedom, hence also with the debtor's freedom, in accordance with a universal external law: thus right and the authority to apply coercion mean one and the same thing.

The law of reciprocal coercion, which is necessarily consonant with the freedom of everyone within the principle of universal freedom, is in a sense the construction of the concept of right: that is, it represents this concept in pure a priori intuition by analogy with the possibility of free movement of bodies within the law of the equality of action and reaction. Just as the qualities of an object of pure mathematics cannot be directly deduced from the concept but can only be discovered from its construction, it is not so much the concept of right but rather a general, reciprocal and uniform coercion, subject to universal laws and harmonizing with the concept itself, which makes any representation of the concept possible. But while this concept of dynamics (i.e., that of the equality of action and reaction) is based upon a purely formal concept of pure mathematics (e.g. of geometry), reason has taken care that the understanding is likewise as fully equipped as possible with a priori intuitions for the construction of the concept of right.

In geometry, the term 'right' (rectum), in the sense of 'straight', can be used either as the opposition of 'curved' or of 'oblique'. In the first sense, it applies to a line whose intrinsic nature is such that there can be only one of its kind between two given points. But in the second sense, it applies to an angle between two intersecting or coincident lines whose nature is such that there can be only one of its kind (a right angle) between the given lines. The perpendicular line which forms a right angle will not incline more to one side than to the other, and will divide the area on either side of it into two equal parts. By this analogy, the theory of right will also seek an assurance that each individual receives (with mathematical precision) what is his due. This cannot be expected of ethics, however, for it cannot refuse to allow some room for exceptions (latitudinem) (pp 132-135).

Note: as there may appear to be error in spelling this is reproducing Kant's edited material. I would like to locate his continuance with equivocal right: "equity and the right of necessity" and the first section of The Metaphysical Elements of Right, where Kant deduces property ownership as direct, indirect, and his idea of "original communal possession of the soil".

ADDENDUM 2

The Metaphysics of Morals
The Theory of Right, Part II: Public Right

Section 1: Political Right

(Page 43) Public right is the sum total of those laws which require to be made universally public in order to produce a state of right. It is, therefore, a system of laws for a people, i.e., an aggregate of human beings, or for an aggregate of peoples. Since these individuals or peoples must influence one another, they need to live in a state of right under a unifying will: that is, they require a constitution in order to enjoy their rights.

A condition in which the individual members of a people are related to each other in this way is said to be a civil one (status civilis), and when considered as a whole in relation to its own members, it is called a state (civitas). Since the state takes the form of a union created by the common interest of everyone in living in a state of right, it is called a commonwealth (res publica latius sic dicta). In relation to other peoples, however, it is simply called a power (potential, hence the word 'potentate'), and if it claims to be united by heredity, it may also call itself a congeneric nation (gens). Within the general concept of public right, we must therefore include not only political right but also international right (ius gentium). And since the earth's surface is not only infinite but limited by its own configuration, these two concepts taken together necessarily lead to the idea of an international political right (ius gentium) or a cosmopolitan right (ius cosmopoliticum). Consequently, if even only one of these three possible forms of rightful state lacks a principle which limits external freedom by means of laws, the structure of all the rest must inevitably be undermined, and finally collapse.

(Page 44) Experience teaches us the maxim that human beings act in a violent and malevolent manner, and that they tend to fight among themselves until an external coercive legislation supervenes. But it is not experience or any kind of factual knowledge which makes public legal coercion necessary. On the contrary, even if we imagine men to be as benevolent and law-abiding as we pleas, the a priori rational idea of a non-lawful state will still tell us that before a public and legal state is established, individual men, peoples and states can never be secure against acts of violence from one another, since each will have his own right to do what seems right and good to him, independently of the opinion of others. Thus, the first decision the individual is obliged to make, if he does not wish to renounce all concepts of right, will be to adopt the principle that one must abandon the state of nature in which everyone follows his own desires, and unite with everyone else (with whom he cannot avoid having intercourse) in order to submit external, public and lawful coercion. He must accordingly enter into a state wherein that which is to recognised as belonging to each person is allotted to him by law and guaranteed to him by an adequate power (which is not his own, but external to him). In other words, he should, at all costs, enter into a state of civil society.

The state of nature need not necessarily be a state of injustice (iniustus) merely because those who live in it treat one another solely in terms of the amount of power they possess. But it is a state devoid of justice (status iustitia vacuus), for if a dispute over rights (ius controversum) occurs in it, there is no competent judge to pronounce legally valid decisions. Anyone may use this force to impel the others to abandon this state for a state of right. For although each individual's concept of right may imply that an external object can be acquired by occupation or by contract, this acquisition is only provisional until it has been sanctioned by a public law, since it is not determined by any public (distributive) form of justice and is not guaranteed by any institution empowered to exercise this right.

If no one were willing to recognize any acquisition as rightful, not even provisionally so, before a civil state had been established, the civil state would itself be impossible. For in relation to their form, the laws relating to property contain exactly the same things in a state of nature as they would prescribe in a civil state, in so far as we conceive of this state only in terms of concepts of pure reason. The only difference is that in the second case, the conditions under which the laws are applied (in accordance with distributive justice) are given. Thus if there were not even a provisional system of external property in the state of nature, there would not be any rightful duties in it either, so that there could not be any commandment to abandon it.

BIBLIOGRAPHY

Arnold, M. 2010. Stakeholder Dialogues for Sustaining Cultural Change. International Studies of Management & Organization, 40(3), 61-77. Retrieved on January 25, 2013, from http://ehis.ebscohost.com/eds/detail?sid=85142774-2d8c-4996-be92-efd9e5815eb9%40sessionmgr112&vid=1&hid=117&bdata=JnNpdGU9ZWRzLWxpdmUmc2NvcGU9c2l0ZQ%3d%3d#db=buh&AN=54288564

Assessing a small organization. (2006). Retrieved from the David Hutton Associates Website: http://www.dhutton.com/news/small_orgs.html

Awadzi Calloway, J. D. 2010. Performance implications of emotional intelligence and transformational leadership: Toward the development of a self-efficacious military leader. (Ph.D. 3413132), Capella University, United States – Minnesota. Retrieved in January 2013, from https://login.ctu.idm.oclc.org/?url=http://search.proquest.com/docview/746606144?accountid=26967ABI/INFORM Complete; ProQuest Dissertations & Theses (PQDT) database

Batorski, M.M. (2012). Developing situation awareness capacity to improve executive judgment and decision-making under stress. (Ed.D. 3503800), Pepperdine University, United States – California. Retrieved on February 27, 2013, from https://login.ctu.idm/oclc.org/url=http://search.proquest.com/docview/1010283532?accountid=26967 ProQuest Dissertations & Theses (PQDT) database

Beedie, C.J., & Lane, A.M. 2012. The Role of Glucose in Self-Control: Another Look at the Evidence and an Alternative Conceptualization. Personality and Social Psychology Review, 16(2), 143-153. Doi: 10.1177/1088868311419817. Retrieved on November 11, 2012, from http://psr.sagepub.com/content/16/2/143.abstract

Bem D. J. 2011. Feeling the future: experimental evidence for anomalous retroactive influences on cognition and affect. Retrieved on February 18, 2013, from http://dbem.ws/FeelingFuture.pdf

Block, P. (2011). Flawless Consulting: A Guide to Getting Your Expertise Used. San Francisco, CA: Jossey-Bass.

Campbell, W., and Campbell, S.M. (2009). On the Self-regulatory Dynamics Created by the Peculiar Benefits and Costs of Narcissism: A Contextual Reinforcement Model and Examination of Leadership. Self & Identity, 8(2/3), 214-232. Doi:10.1080/152988608 02505129. Retrieved on May 2, 2014, from: http://eds.a.ebscohost.com.proxy.cecybrary.com/ehost/

pdfviewer/pdfviewer?sid=c4b8db12-705e-4943-8af9-4ab17dc1b186%40ses
sionmgr4003&vid=9&hid=4203

Cannon, W. M. (1972). Organization design: Shaping structure to strategy. Mckinsey Quarterly, 9(1), 25–32

Case Study: Kaiser Permanente's Healthy Approach to Change. (2008). Training, 45(6), 19. Retrieved February 2, 2014, from http://eds.b.ebscohost. com.ctu.idm.oclc.org/edsdetail?sid=19fce543-ea29-4601-ab1b-7a54927b d5fa%40sessionmgr198&vid=8&hid=102&bdata=JnNpdGU9ZWRzLWx pdmUmc2NvcGU9c2l0ZQ%3d%3d#db=buh&AN=33312499

CITI Program, June 14, 2012. Collaborative Institutional Training Initiative. Retrieved on November 3, 2012, from https://www.citiprogram.org/members/learnersII/moduletext.asp?strKeyID=EE2AF2BC-59E9-493B-9469-4CE8A85721BC-13564635&module= 1321

Collins, J. (2001). The Level 5 Leader. In W. E. Natemeyer & P. Hersey (Eds). Classics of Organizational Behavior (fourth edition). Long Grove, IL: Waveland Press, Inc.

Cooper, R. & Markus, M.L. (July 15, 1995). Human reengineering. Retrieved on February 5, 2014 from http://sloanreview.mit.edu/article/human-reengineering/

Creswell, J. W. 2009. Research design, qualitative, quantitative, and mixed methods approaches (3 ed.). Thousand Oaks, California: Sage.

Cummings, T.G. & Worley, C.G. (2009). Organizational Development & Change (9 ed.). South-Western, Ohio: Centage.

de Vries, M., Witteman, C. L. M., Holland, R. W. & Dijksterhuis, A. 2010. The Unconscious Thought Effect in Clinical Decision Making: An Example in Diagnosis. Medical Decision Making, 30(5), 578-581. Doi: 10.1177/0272989x09360820. Retrieved on February 18, 2013, from http://pps.sagepub.com/content/1/2/95.abstract

DeWall, C.N., Baumeister, R.F., Gailliot, M.T., & Maner, J.K. 2008. Depletion Makes the Heart Grow Less Helpful: Helping as a Function of Self-Regulatory Energy and Genetic Relatedness. Personality and Social Psychology Bulletin, 34(12), 1653-1662. Doi: 10.1177/0146167208323981. Retrieved on November 11, 2012, from http://psp.sagepub.com/content/34/12/1653.abstract

Dickerson, S.S., Gable, S.L., Irwin, M.R., Aziz, N., & Kemeny, M.E. 2009. Social-Evaluative Threat and Proinflammatory Cytokine Regulation: An Experimental Laboratory Investigation. Psychological Science, 20(10), 1237-1244. Doi: 10.1111/j.1467-9280.2009.02437.x. Retrieved on November 13, 2012, from http://pss.sagepub.com/content/20/10/1237.abstract

Dijksterhuis, A. & Nordgren, L. F. 2006. A Theory of Unconscious Thought. Perspectives on Psychological Science, 1(2), 95-109. Doi: 10.1111/j.1745-6916.2006.00007.x. Retrieved on February 18, 2013, from http://pps.sagepub.com/content/1/2/95.abstract

DuBois, R. (2012). Interview with researcher's and author's sibling

DuBois, S. (July, 2013). Lymphatic management. Institute of Strategic and International Studies (ISIS). Presenter: Key West Symposium (since renamed their organization for political aversion).

Edmondson, A., & McManus, S. (2007). Methodological Fit In Management Field Research. Academy of Management Review, 32(4), 1155-1179

Fautua, D.T., & Schatz, S. 2012. Cognitive Readiness and the Challenge of Institutionalizing the "New" Versus "News". Journal of Cognitive Engineering and Decision Making, 6(3), 276-298. Doi: 10.1177/1555343412444366. Retrieved on November 21, 2012, from http://edm.sagepub.com/ content/6/3/276.abstract

Feldman, D.C. 2004. What are We Talking About When We Talk About Theory? Journal of Management, 30(5), 565-567. Doi: 10.1016/j.jm.2004.05.001

Frame, J.D. (2013). Framing Decisions: Decision Making that Accounts for Irrationality, People, and Constraints. San Francisco, CA: Jossey-Bass.

Gailliot, M.T. & Baumeister, R.F. 2007. The Physiology of Willpower: Linking Blood Glucose to Self-Control. Personality and Social Psychology Review, 11(4), 303-327. Doi: 10.1177/1088868307303030. Retrieved on November 11, 2012, from http://psr.sagepub.com/ content/11/4/303.abstract

Galbraith, J., Downey, D., and Kates, A. (2002). A Hands-On Guide for Leaders at All Levels: Designing Dynamic Organizations. N.Y., N.Y.: AMACOM.

Gardner, W.L. & Cleavenger, D. 1998. The Impression Management Strategies Associated with Transformational Leadership at the World-Class Level: A Psycho-historical Assessment.

Management Communication Quarterly, 12(1), 3-41. Doi: 10.1177/0893318998121001. Retrieved on November 9, 2012, from http://mcq.sagepub.com/content/12/1/3.abstract

Gerhardt, M., Ashenbaum, B., & Newman, W.R. 2009. Understanding the Impact of Proactive Personality on Job Performance: The Roles of Tenure and Self-Management. Journal of Leadership & Organizational Studies, 16(1), 61-72. Doi: 10.1177/154805 1809334192. Retrieved on November 4, 2012, from http://jlo.sagepub.com/content/16/1/61.abstract

Glatthorn, A. A. & Joyner, R. L. 2005. Writing the Winning Thesis or Dissertation: A Step-by-Step Guide (2 ed.). Thousand Oaks, California: Sage.

Gonzalez, L. 2008. Everyday Survival, Why Smart People Do Stupid Things. NY, NY: W. W. Norton & Company.

Holman, P., Devane, T., & Cady, S. (eds.) (2007). The Change Handbook: The Definitive Resource on Today's Best Methods for Engaging Whole Systems. San Francisco, CA: Berrett-Koehler Publishers, Inc.

Horn, L. 2013. MGMT805, Class lecture. Retrieved archive on January 14, 2013, from https://campus.ctuonline.edu/pages/MainFrame.aspx?Content Frame=/Classroom/course.aspx?Class=356790 HYPERLINK "https://

campus.ctuonline.edu/pages/MainFrame.aspx?ContentFrame=/Class room/course.aspx?Class=356790 HYPERLINK

Hyland, M.E. 2002. The Intelligent Body and its Discontents. Journal of Health Psychology, 7(1), 21-32. Doi: 10.1177/1359105302007001649. Retrieved on November 11, 2012, from http://hpq.sagepub.com/content/7/1/21.abstract

Inzlicht, M. & Schmeichel, B.J. 2012. What Is Ego Depletion? Toward a Mechanistic Revision of the Resource Model of Self-Control. Perspectives on Psychological Science, 7(5), 450-463. Doi: 10.1177/1745691612454134. Retrieved on November 11, 2012, from http://pps.sagepub.com/content/7/5/450.abstract

Jaffe, E. 2007. Mirror neurons are how we reflect on behavior. Article from the Association for Psychological Science. Retrieved on March 21, 2011, from http://www.psychologicalscience.org/observer/get Article.cfm?id=2167

Johnson, A. M. 2011. The Impact of Managerial Emotional Intelligence Perceptions on the Occupational Well-Being of Employees in a Police Department. (Ph.D. 3482199), Walden University, United States – Minnesota. Retrieved on February 18, 2013, from https://login.ctu.idm/oclc.org/?url=http://search.proquest.com/docview/909529100?accountid=26967 ProQuest Dissertations & Theses (PQDT) database

Kabacoff, R. I., (2008). Issues of global and local norm use in assessments of motivation. Doi: 10.1080/15305050802435128

Kesting, P., Smolinski, R., & Speakman, J.I. (November 19, 2010). Conflict in organizations: the role of routine. Retrieved on December 14, 2012, from http://papers.ssrn.com/sol3/papers.cfm?abstract_id=1741904 or http://dx.doi.org/10.2139/ssrn.1741904

Long, T. (2012). Constituting the stress response: Collaborative networks and the elucidation of the pituitary-adrenal cortical system, 1930s-1960s. (Ph.D. 3492584), The Johns Hopkins University, United States – Maryland. Retrieved on February 25, 2013, from https://login.ctu.idm/oclc.org/?url=http://search.proquest.com/docview/918183063?accountid=26967 ProQuest Dissertations & Theses (PQDT) database

Lubbers, R. W. (2003). Self-efficacy and affective well-being among young workers: Examining job quality as an antecedent of employee health and performance outcomes. Retrieved on December 16, 2013, from https://login.ctu.idm/oclc.org/?url=http://search.proquest.com/docview/305244605?accountid=26967

Maynard, E. (August 3, 2014). Interview on "Future-Science Education". Retrieved on October 4, 2014, from www.arcoscielos.com

McNaught, J.E. (2012). How Baby-Boomers experienced leaders use intuition in decision making. Psychological Science, 1(2), 95-109. Doi: 10.1111/j.1745-6916.2006.00007. Retrieved on February 18, 2013, from https://login.ctu.idm/oclc.org/?url=http://search.proquest.com/docview/

1020616421?accountid=26967 ProQuest Dissertations & Thesis (PQDT) database

Mintzberg, H. (2009). Managing. San Francisco, CA: Berrett-Koehler Publishers, Inc.

Northouse, P. G. 2010. Leadership, Theory and Practice (5 ed). Thousand Oaks, CA: Sage. Pees, R.C. & Shoop, G.H. (2009). Organizational consciousness. Journal of Health Organization and Management, 23(5), 505-521

Organizational assessment. (2013). Retrieved from The Forbes Funds Web site: http://forbesfunds.org/tools/building-management-capacity/organiza tional-assessment

Pees, R.C. & Shoop, G.H. (2009). Organizational consciousness. Journal of Health Organization and Management, 23(5), 505-521Phillips, E.L. 2011. Resilience, Mental Flexibility, and Cortisol Response to the Montreal Imaging Stress Task in Unemployed Men. (Ph.D. 3459041), University of Michigan, United States -- Michigan. Retrieved on February 20, 2013, from https://login.ctu.idm/oclc.org/?url=http://search.proquest.com/docview/ 873449650?accountid=26967

Reiss, H. (ed.) (1992). Kant Political Writings: Cambridge Texts In The History of Political Thought. NY, NY: Cambridge University Press.

Sadri, N. 2008. The knockout mouse model reveals the multi-faceted functions of AUF1. (Ph.D. 3332222), New York University, United States – New York. Retrieved on February 25, 2013, from https://login.ctu.idm/oclc. org/?url=http://search.proquest.com/docview/908974952?accountid= 26967 ProQuest Dissertations & Theses (PQDT) database

Shaffer, J.A. & Postlethwaite, B.E. (2012). A matter of context: A meta-analytic investigation of the relative validity of contextualized and non-contextualized personality measures. Personnel Psychology, 65, 445-494. Retrieved on May 4, 2014, from onlinelibrary.wiley.com/doi/10.1111/j.1744-6570.2012.01250.x/pdf

Sharma, A. K., & Talwar, B. 2007. Evolution of "universal business excellence model" incorporating vedic philosophy. Measuring Business Excellence, 11(3), 4-20. Doi: 10.1108 /13683040710820719. Retrieved on June 10, 2012, from http://www.emeraldinsight.com.ctu.idm.oclc.org/journals.htm? issn=1368-3047&volume=11&issue=3&articleid=1621803

Shepard, D.A., & Sutcliffe, K.M. (2011). Inductive top-down theorizing: A source of new theories of organization. Academy of Management Review. V. 36, No. 2, 361-380. Retrieved on February 25, 2013.

Sutton, R.I. & Staw, B.M. 1995. Administrative Science Quarterly, 40(3), 371-384

Sznycer, D. 2010. Cognitive adaptations for calibrating welfare tradeoff motivations, with special reference to the emotion of shame. (Ph.D. 3439655). University of California, Santa Barbara, United States – California.

Retrieved in January, 2013, from https://login.ctu.idm/oclc.org/?url=http://search.proquest.com/docview/851696213?accountid=26967 ProQuest Dissertations & Theses (PQDT) database

Tjosvold, D. 1987. Participation: A Close Look at Its Dynamics. Journal of Management, 13(4), 739-750. Doi: 10.1177/014920638701300413. Retrieved on February 18, 2013, from http://jom.sagepub.com/content/13/4/739.abstract

Tullett, A.M., Teper, R., & Inzlicht, M. 2011. Confronting Threats to Meaning: A New Framework for Understanding Responses to Unsettling Events. Perspectives on Psychological Science, 6(5), 447-453. Doi: 10.1177/1745691611414588. Retrieved in January 2013, from http://pps.sagepub.com/content/6/5/447.abstract

Vance, D. E., Roberson, A. J., McGuinness, T. M., & Fazeli, P. L. 2010. How neuroplasticity and cognitive reserve protect cognitive functioning. Journal of Psychosocial Nursing & Mental Health Services, 48(4), 23-30. Doi: 10.3928/02793695-20100302-01. Retrieved on January 14, 2013, from http://search.ebscohost.com/login.Aspx?direct=true&db=rzh&AN=2010632724&site=ehost-live&scope=site

VanHoose, L. D. (2011). Cardiac dysfunction in the ZDF rat: Possible mechanisms and benefits of exercise. (Ph.D. 3481293), University of Kansas, United States – Kansas. Retrieved on February 24, 2013, from https://login.ctu.idm/oclc.org/?url=http://search.proquest.com/docview/905591136?accountid=26967 ProQuest Dissertations & Theses (PQDT) database

Vogelsang (ed) et. al., J. (© 2013). Handbook for strategic HR: best practices in organization development from the od network. [Books24x7 version] Available from http://common.books24x7.com.ctu.idm.oclc.org/toc.aspx?bookid=47768

Vul, Edward, Harris, Christine, Winkielman, Piotr, & Pashler, Harold. (2009). Puzzlingly High Correlations in fMRI Studies of Emotion, Personality, and Social Cognition. Perspectives on Psychological Science, 4(3), 274-290. Doi: 10.1111/j.1745-6924.2009.01125.x

Wade, J. (2008). Employees First Pay Off. HR Magazine, 53(12), 40. Retrieved on February 3, 2014 from http://eds.b.ebscohost.com.ctu.idm.oclc.org/eds/detail?vid=39

Werther, W. (1999). Structure-driven strategy and virtual organization design. Business Horizons, 42(2), 13

World Bank Institute presentation (October 26, 2003). Illustration retrieved on March 18, 2014, from http://www.impactalliance.org/file_download.php?location=S_U HYPERLINK 12804300851The_Rapid_Results_Approach_PPT_WBIFP.ppt

Zender, R. & Olshansky, E. (2012). The Biology of Caring: Researching the Healing Effects of Stress Response Regulation Through Relational Engagement. Biological Research For Nursing, 14(4), 419-430. Doi: 10.1177/1099800412450505. Retrieved in January 2013, from http://brn. sagepub.com/content/14/4/419.abstract